The DEATH SQUAD

by

Trey Haynes

Acknowledgments

I acknowledge those who helped inspire me on my scripts and stories, as well as provided ideas and assistance. Head editor, Mike Stutzman, editing, Kynda Yates, cover and illustrations, Joe Turner and layout Paul Hail. I would also like to thank for their help: Dewayne Henagar, Beverly Emmett, Chris Chaplin, Dixie Jordan, Andrew Lim, Steve Thompson, Trudy Rogers, Tamela Ekstrom, Robin Branham, Julie Bartness

My friends and partners at Print Imaging, and, of course, Donna and Bob McKeegan for all their hard work with anything ever asked of them. Thank you to my parents, Jim and Peggy Haynes, sister, Cori Osborn, brother, Mike Haynes, niece, Sarah Stephens, as well as extended family, Russ Letchford, Richard McMillan, Hugh, Kathleen, and Cory Wheelus, the Ryans and the Seegers.

I would also like to acknowledge friends: Scott Danemiller, Bryan Matula, Dan Dooling, James Laing, Stace Harris, Jeff Glass, Troy Redmon, Jimmy Cook, Tom Skinner, Jeff Stoabs, Jay Collins, Robert Paiva, Mark Hasting, John Conley, Bridget Young, Greig Lumsden and of course the Schlageters. The Beau's Wine Bin group, 66' Bowl group, and my friends at the INTEGRIS Healthline and One Call. Lastly, I'd like to acknowledge a friend who always made me laugh, did not take anything seriously, and will always be missed, Rick Bluhm.

ADMIT ONE

The DEATH SQUAD

THE DEATH MOBILE

A crow was perched on a solid concrete tombstone in a dreary cemetery and opened its beak. KAAAAAA! KAAAAAA!

The earth shook and rumbled below as if something were desperately trying to break through and the crow flew off, disappearing into the murky night.

A tall, cross-shaped gravestone fell to the side as a wooden coffin burst partially through the earth and a skeletal arm plopped out. The gravestone and earth dropped into a large hole in the ground and a shiny, black hearse which was referred to as the ***Death Mobile,*** violently ripped through the earth from below. It knocked headstones to the side, throwing dirt and bones in the air and clear of its path. The gargoyle hood ornament with red beady eyes screamed at the sky, and then spit out dirt and a couple of small pebbles. A low, booming man's voice was heard inside the car:

"NOBODY GETS OUT ALIVE!"

The Death Mobile stalled and died. Grumbling was heard amongst the passengers inside, especially after the bold announcement of impending death that typically made them all giddy with excitement.

A brief moment passed as a key turned in the ignition but no luck followed by another sigh. A tired, sweaty hunchback gravedigger, who had worked all night, looked up from a grave he was digging and shook his head. "Bring it in and I'll have it checked."

The engine turned over and screamed.

Lightning from the Heavens fired high above and extended its fingers across the sky.

The ***Death Squad*** consisted of four dark angels who set out on their mission of finishing off those who had eluded death or their time of expiration, as opposed to the good angels who saved lost souls. They of course wanted desperately to finish these last few missions so they could graduate up to eternal bliss and get their "good wings". Their luck had been sour up to this point, just like in life, but they forged on, despite the setbacks.

Swamp, Slidell, Louisiana

The swamp, loaded with twenty-foot tall cypress trees, frogs the size of a football, and the muddy waters of the Mississippi river, hid a cabin where gunshots rang out.

Two drunk rednecks in dirty overalls- Billy Bob and Billy Joe- stood in the middle of a wood cabin with shotguns, enjoying their night as they shot unsuspecting swamp rats. It was a hobby of theirs that they played when not gigging frogs in the swamp and it led to many visits to the emergency room.

They looked in every direction in the cabin, which was almost bare except for an old, brown, moldy couch in the middle and a kitchen counter top littered with animal skins, frog legs, cheap beer and potato chips.

"That's fourteen, Billy Joe!" Billy Bob bragged.

A line of rats were hung in the corner of the room as one rat snuck away under Billy Joe's watchful eye. He gulped down his beer and tossed the can in the corner with a pile of others. Billy Joe slyly pointed to the other corner of the room, spotting his target.

"Don't look now, but we got a critter at, oh, bout' nine o'clock."

Dumbfounded, Billy Bob looked all around, including up, as he swung the shotgun wildly, not wanting to miss one. Billy Joe pointed again.

"Over there, Billy Bob. Durn."

Orco, large and an easy-going angel of death, slid in next to Billy Bob. "Any last words?"

Billy Bob studied him and wondered how he got in without either of them noticing. "You aint' a cousin, is ya?"

Orco ran a comb through his wavy, black hair and chuckled as he gave them a "you should know better" fatherly look while he waved his finger and pulled a scroll out of his black leather jacket.

"You huckleberries have known for years not to play with guns."

Billy Bob raised his hand like a scorned school student. "He durn near shot me in the balls yesterday."

"Well, he shot me in the ear last week." Billy Joe complained while tugging at the little flesh that remained of his right ear.

Orco's demeanor changed to all business as he was on a tight schedule, "-and as a representative of the dead, I am to inform you that we are here to make sure that you don't cheat death again and alter your destiny. Your expiration is past due and-"

Orco tucked the scroll away and put it in his back pocket. He'd been through the routine many times before.

Orco glanced over at Perneum who stood at the door holding a butcher's knife.

Perneum or "Per", was an angry dwarf with beady red eyes from England in the 1600's, and Lucifer's right hand man before joining the Death Squad. He lived for this. Sometimes it was the chase, but usually it was the art of finishing off some poor soul who thought they've cheated death and were destined to live forever.

Orco pointed the rifle a little to the left and it fired, ricocheting off a frying pan and hitting Billy Bob squarely in the chest. Billy Bob staggered a little on his feet as Orco held the rifle with one hand and a mirror with the other, while looking backward and squinting. He shot again and Billy Joe dropped to the floor while Orco pumped his arm. "Bulls eye!"

Billy Bob touched his heaving chest, spewing blood and didn't quite understand. "The heck was that fer?" His heavy frame fell forward but his cloudy, white spirit promptly stood back up.

Billy Joe's and Billy Bob's ghosts walked past the two other ghoulish, dark angel characters who pointed to a light outside the cabin door. Billy Bob grabbed a half-empty beer on the way out and took a long swig.

"BURP! You ain't gettin' out of buying the next round!"

Beer ran through his spirit and onto the floor as Billy Bob punched Billy Joe in the spiritual arm. "Yor' makin' a mess."

Orco walked past the two remaining members of the Death Squad.

Artesia was a tall, skinny, Gothic type with long stringy black hair and pale, placid skin. He quietly walked the streets of Salem until he was believed to be a witch and was brought before a jury and hung… Then burned… Then doused in water to put out the flames and burned again.

Justice was swift and brutal during the witch trial period in Salem.

Pierrot was a leathery, scarred female Viking with fiery red hair and pigtails peaking out from under her helmet. She carried a large sledge hammer and had torched many ex-boyfriends back in the eleventh century.

With forked tails dragging behind, they hoped the worst was behind them. A job well done and off to their next assignment.

Greenville Speedway, Greenville, South Carolina

A warm breeze passed over the grandstand as people rushed to their seats with their nachos, sodas and beers in hand. A local daredevil on a motorcycle revved his engine a few times to tease the crowd. A line of vans with ramps on both ends awaited him. Adoring fans cheered and snapped photographs as the announcer in a tan, suede jacket leaned close to the microphone. "The Great One will attempt a world record and another death-defying leap!"

The crowd went wild and the daredevil waved at them before slapping his helmet shield down.

Orco, Perneum, Artesia and Pierrot stood by the ramp on the opposite end with mechanic's gear on. "Death defying?" Orco mentioned as this was nothing to him. Orco tried jumping over a canyon on a motorcycle back in the fifties when he hung with Kerouac the poet.

Perneum looked over a list, as he ran his fingers along the names and back at Orco. "Checked it twice, he's overdue."

The daredevil looked back at the cheering crowd one last time before he revved his engine and took off with rubber smoking behind him. Orco and the guys moved the landing ramp to the side as he went airborne.

Artesia wiped off his hands and turned to Orco. "Who's next?"

"I think a hospital in New York and a cookout in Texas and we're done,"

The screaming motorcycle flew past them and the SOUND OF METAL SCREECHING against the pavement was followed by a small explosion. Perneum marked a small skull and crossbones next to the daredevil's name as Orco led them away. "It won't be long and we can do away with that thing."

Pierrot was not as convinced as she pulled back her hair and put small leather straps around the bright red pigtails. "Yeah, I've heard that a few times."

The daredevil staggered to them. His helmet was mangled and

an arm was badly bent behind him. Orco pointed to a bright light in the distance.

"Just follow the light."

"I still have another show to do," the daredevil told him, looking down with no regard for his broken legs. Orco pointed him to the light. "Just follow the light, Sir."

The daredevil dragged himself towards the light, tripped, and crawled on.

Belleview Hospital, Queens, New York

The smell of disinfectant filled the air as the Death Squad stood in the foyer of the large, aging hospital. Orco slapped his hands together. "Let's desecrate the living."

The overweight security guard clutched his nightstick and walked to the group with a swagger. "I don't see nothing wrong with you guys and we aint' got room, so beat it."

Orco nodded at Artesia, who grabbed the security guard and the others ran down the hospital halls. The guard blew his whistle.

"Hey! Hey! Stop them!"

Doctors and nurses were gathered around a man on the operating table as the heart monitor beeped loudly. The doctor reached out and without looking he demanded, "Heart." He reached back as a plastic model was handed to him. He laid it aside. "Heart!!" A Mr. Potato Head toy was handed to him. He held it out. "What the hell is this!?" The doctor turned and Pierrot ran out of the room as the heart monitor beeped rapidly.

"He's going into cardiac arrest!" The doctor scrambled to save the man as Pierrot was already safely out of the room.

Perneum ran down a hall pushing a screaming elderly lady in a wheelchair. He let go and the wheelchair and woman with flailing arms went banging through double doors into an operating room. Perneum grabbed a large knife and eagerly ran down another hall.

An old woman in a nightgown held her lotto card as she laid snuggly in bed and watched television. The card was jerked out of her hand.

Orco held the card and looked at the television set that flashed the winning numbers and then pulled the blanket comfortably over her. "You know you shouldn't be straining your eyes, Doctor (he picked up her chart and read the doctor's name instead) Mafood Mushy Mushy." She looked up at him confused but with tender care. "Stop being silly and give that back."

She reached for the lotto card as the final numbers 12 and 17 flashed across the bottom of the screen. Orco gave her a shocked look and trembled with the card in his hand. "Can it be?"

The elderly lady reached further for the ticket. "Well, what is it? Three out of five? That sometimes pays-"

Orco's eyes got wide as he started in again. "You, Misses Mushy Mushy!... HAVE JUST WON SIXTY FIVE MILLION… err, BILLION DOLLARS!" He jumped up and down. She grabbed her chest and keeled over as Orco tossed the ticket aside and left.

Back at the hospital cafeteria, Perneum chased people around the tables with the large knife.

Security guards beat on Artesia with clubs at the entrance as he tried to stall them as long as possible with minimal bruising. One guard even maced him as he clutched his face in agonizing pain.

Orco's black leather jacket swung from side to side as he strutted down the hall. He slicked back his hair with his hand and without looking, switched pill bottles on the counter. He stopped, remembering something, and walked in a patient's room.

The doctor was observing a patient as Orco looked over his shoulder.

"Uh, excuse me?"

The doctor abruptly stopped. "I am with a patient." Orco took a step closer and tapped on the doctor's shoulder.

"I've just had a real bad sore throat, lately. Mind looking at it?" The aggravated doctor quickly turned and leered at Orco. "I only have a minute." He hastily looked into Orco's ear and a yellowish eyeball glowered back at him. The surprised doctor took a step back, shook his head and then grabbed a tongue depressor. "Open your mouth and say, ahhhhhh." He peered inside Orco's mouth. Little green monsters fought with each other and scowled back at the doctor who jumped back again. "Aaarrrgggggghhh!" The doctor screamed as Orco nodded his head with grave concern. "I knew it wasn't good."

The stunned and speechless doctor pointed at the medicine cabinet.

"Thanks, Doc." Orco took the stack of pills, gobbled them up and walked out.

Back in the parking lot, Orco pulled on the bones that served as door handles as the guys jumped into the Death Mobile.

A lanky man in jeans walked to the car holding a cigarette. "Hey buddy, can I get a light?" The man held his cigarette out and Orco gladly obliged, blowing a large flame out of his mouth. The man's hair smoked and his face was charred black as there was nothing left of the cigarette.

"Thanks, friend. No need for that laser hair removal I was going in for."

The man walked off and Orco hopped in but quickly back out of the Death Mobile and opened the back door. He waited with his hands on his hips as the spirit of the little old lady slowly floated out. Orco led her to a light. "Just follow the light and you'll be okay." She waved the ticket and he gave her a faint smile. "I know you won. Now go on." The gargoyle hood ornament had a cigarette in its mouth and blew out small puffs of smoke.

The group sat in their usual spots with Perneum in the front seat as Orco drove toward the exit. Perneum slammed an eight-track tape of disco in the stereo and then shook his fist at the hospital.

Orco steered the Death Mobile out of the parking lot and accidentally ran over a man who was tying his shoe."Was he on the list?" Orco asked. Perneum held up the list and looked it over before flipping a couple of pages and locking his eyes on the name.

"Not for a couple of years."

Orco slapped the steering wheel. "Ahead of schedule!"

The group smiled at each other for a job well done as they fully expected to get their good wings after one more assignment in Texas.

Texas State Penitentiary, Longview, Texas

The sky was heavy with streaks of black and gray. Lightning struck, illuminating the endless fields and prison below.

Artesia, Perneum and Pierrot landed on the wall of the prison as Orco was forced to crawl up the side due to the difficulty of flying with his heavy weight. He caught his breath as he kneeled in front of the group. "This is the last one. Let's not screw it up."

"I've heard that before." Artesia glumly responded when-
SHOTGUN BLAST!

The impact sent Artesia flying over the side as an aging guard patrolling one of the towers and wearing large horn-rimmed glasses, squinted to see what he hit. "Damn crows." He walked back to patrol the other side of the night of the much publicized execution. Orco looked down below where Artesia gave a thumbs up. His wing smoked from the shotgun blast as he laid on his back.

"I'll just meet you inside."

Inside the prison, water dripped from rusty pipes that wound around the ceiling as a warm breeze flowed through the cells. The smell of death filled the air as prisoners waited patiently for the ultimate sentence of one of their evil own.

Prison guards strapped down the greasy convict, Clown Killer Edwards, in the electric chair. Edwards noticed Pierrot's green tail, wagging under her guard uniform. Without the use of his hands, which were strapped into the chair of death, he gestured as much as he could. "Hey! UH-"

ZAP! Sparks flew from wires dangling from the chair. Edwards' hair stood on end as Orco, also dressed as another guard, flipped the switch, then quickly put it back down. Orco threw his hands up.

"Just testing."

Artesia, wearing a black robe and hood, walked in with the priest. The guards stepped away as the short Texas governor, wearing a brown polyester suit and cowboy hat, addressed a room full of angry clowns, telling them to calm down.

The governor looked toward Edwards. "I would like to ask ya, why did you do it?" Edwards looked over the sneering clowns; their white make-up was melting in the sweltering, unventilated observation room. "Cause, I didn't think they was funny." He broke out in maniacal laughter. The clowns began beating on the glass wall and shook their fists as one tied a balloon up to resemble a middle finger. The governor tried to quell the noise. "Okay! Calm down, you clowns!"

He looked toward a snide Edwards. "Do you have any last words, convicted Clown Killer Edwards?" A clown held up a picture of one of Edwards' victims. The picture revealed only legs and large clown shoes that protruded out from beneath a house.

"So, you finally caught up with me." He taunted the guards.

"Seems like I've used up all my nine lives. ***I'LL SEE YOU IN HELL!!"***

Everyone looked at each other. A confused clown spoke out to the others.

"Uh, who's he talking to?" They all nodded their heads and a frustrated Edwards blurted out. "Just get on with it!"

Thunder rang out and Perneum tightened the straps and stared down at Edwards. Edwards grimaced, the electrodes placed securely on his scalp. "I'll be damned if you ain't the ugliest-" Perneum sucker-punched Edwards across the chin and dazed him before he was able to finish. The governor boldly stood in front of the electric chair and turned to Edwards as the cameras began to roll. "No more appeals for you, Edwards. This is it." The governor turned to Orco. "He is straight from hell."

"Nah, just a cheap imitation." Orco scoffed.

Thunder roared outside and the lights flickered off and on. Ready to get this party started, the governor stepped away and slapped his hand down like he was starting a fighting cage match.

"LET'S GET IT ON!... Eh, I mean, let's proceed."

The switch was turned up and Edwards' hair fired straight up again and his face lit up, much to the amusement of the Death Squad. Orco held the switch and smiled to himself. "These never get old." The lights went out but immediately came back on. Artesia lit his cigarette off of Edward's forehead as he convulsed violently.

Inmates gripped the bars in their cells and looked out across at each other as more water gushed from the roof and the lights flickered off and on for longer periods of time.

The gauge on the wall showed that the amps were rapidly dropping. The governor, fearful of the most violent inmate the prison had ever housed, took a step back. "What is going on?" The lights went out and the emergency lights immediately came on.

"Check the breaker!!"

The panicked and terrified governor screamed at his maintenance men as he shuffled backward. Edwards ferociously ripped at the leather straps, viciously tearing them from his wrists. Smoke rose from his singed hair.

"Ha! You just cain't kill me! I've got ten lives! Maybe eleven!" Edwards tossed the straps aside and stood over the governor, who cowered in the corner.

"Guards. GUARDS!!" The governor screamed out as lightning struck and illuminated Edwards' demonic grin as he held his fists up. "I'm alive! ALIVE DAMN YOU!!"

BOINK! An inflatable hammer came down on his head. Edwards turned and the clown holding it backed off, pleading with him. "Don't hurt the happy clown… Happy clown." The clown struck a playful pose, which infuriated Edwards more, thinking he was being mocked.

Edwards grabbed the clown by the nose and pulled it back but Orco clamped down on Edwards' wrist.

Perneum was busy putting on plastic gloves and happily whistling to himself as Artesia stretched out his hamstrings and worked his head side to side like a boxer. Pierrot flashed her long, razor sharp fingernails. Orco popped his fingers and grinned. "Our turn now." Orco and the others converged on him, tossing body parts up in the air.

The governor, back on his feet, looked back toward the camera with a stern expression as he straightened his tie. "Let it be known we are tough on crime." Munching and crackling sounded off behind him. He turned back.

"Uh, guys."

Orco held up Edwards' severed arm. The governor turned to the camera man. "You might want to turn that thing off..."

The guys made a short pit stop at the graveyard before celebrating their accomplishments. They were finally ready to get fitted for a new pair of wings. It was time to save souls, who would look to them with a gleaming smile of appreciation as opposed to expressions that were frozen in fear. Time to sit at the right hand of our Father. Time to retire to a palace lined in gold, but for the moment, ninety nine cent beer night at the Rusty Pelican in New Orleans would have to do.

Orco popped a bottle of champagne as Perneum grabbed his briefcase like he was ready to leave. Orco slapped it down immediately. "We'll pack later!" He grabbed the briefcase again and Orco pulled at it but let go. "Ya seem a might attached to that thing."

Perneum started walking away until the guys jumped in the Death Mobile, ready to go celebrate. The hood ornament smoked a cigar and smiled. Orco curiously watched Perneum, who reluctantly tossed the luggage aside and decided to join them. Artesia grabbed a glass and leaned out the window. "Let's celebrate!" Orco slapped Perneum on the shoulder.

"You never leave a man behind! You ain't goin' anywhere yet." He opened the door and Perneum hesitated but gave in and hopped inside the Death Mobile.

Bourbon Street, New Orleans, Louisiana

A colorful, jazzed-up funeral parade moved down the street as the group stood out front and waved their beers while posing for pictures.

"We earned our wings, guys!" Orco cried out and Artesia joined him, wrapping his long, lanky arms around Orco's broad shoulders.

"We did it!"

The night for the Death Squad was a load of fun as they enjoyed as many bars as they could find and even bragged to a few of the locals about their recent accomplishment which, despite how crazy the stories sounded, earned them a few rounds of drinks.

Camera shot- The guys smiling for the camera.
Camera shot- The guys crowding around a woman who teases the guys like she is going to flash them.
Camera shot- Orco holds Perneum in his arms as Pierrot and Artesia pour beer on him.
Camera shot- Blurry vision of someone's pant leg.

Hours later, the party had passed as the guys slept soundly in the middle of the street. THUMP, the morning street cleaner ran over a sprawled out Artesia.

Orco sipped on a beer as he sat on the curb pondering the Death Squad's future. He glanced over at Art who was flattened. "He'll feel that in the morning." Perneum rolled over in the street, garbage stuck to his face. "We have to get back," Orco mentioned, excited to find out the final preparations before crossing over to join the good guys in white.

ALASTOR, THE FALLEN ANGEL

Beverly Hills, California

Palm trees blew mildly in the warm California wind. A large, brick mansion was surrounded by a thick concrete wall which was typical for the large houses in the affluent neighborhood.

A beach ball flew over the wall and hit a guard in the head causing him to spin around and fire his rifle into the air. Another guard looked over, realizing there was no threat and then walked the rest of the sprawling premises.

Inside the mansion a pale, thin butler, who carried no expression on his dapper, long face, walked through a spotless and cold foyer with a tray of wine and glasses. He passed a door and a hand reached out from under the stairs. The butler stepped on the hand, squashed his heel on it, and walked on with perfect posture and chin up with a hint of a smile.

Paintings on the wall scowled at the butler and hissed as he entered a large oak door that opened to a large board room. Red felt lined the walls as marble statues of fallen angels adorned the corners of the spacious room with a high ceiling. Men of different ethnic backgrounds and clothed in dark suits sat around the board room table. Seated at the head of the long table was the most evil angel of all. Alastor, tanned and early 50's with dark black, oily, slicked-back hair and neatly trimmed side burns that came to a point, faced the wall in his black leather chair.

As an angel, he was never cast out but left on his own due to his jealousy of the big guy's powers. He sought out to control souls with evil instead of leading them to a higher, divine power. He found a captive audience on earth, first at Tupperware parties and then graduated up to selling customized lots in Heaven by the acre. After making a fortune, he grabbed his earnings and took advantage of a crippled, California real estate market.

Alastor tapped his cane against the marble floor and the obedient butler quickly went to him with a tray of wine. Alastor took a glass of burgundy and dipped his forked tongue into it, savoring the rich taste. He gave a wink of approval and the butler made his way back to the servant's quarters, promptly stepping on the hand under the stairs again. Armed guards stood in every corner of the room. Alastor continued to face the wall as he addressed the group with a soft but assertive tone. "I feel that it's important that we-"

Young athletic men in bathing suits ran inside. "PARTY!?" One blurted out as another looked around the room extremely disappointed. "Where are the babes, old, decrepit dudes?"

"House next door." Alastor told them as he pointed with hands that were lined with protruding purple veins. "Sorry, dudes," they yelled back running as Alastor waved them off with his bony fingers. "Don't mention it." Alastor paused. "Can we secure the place a wee bit better?... Is that possible?"

Alastor swung around in his chair and smashed his knee on the corner of the marble table. The men at the table uncomfortably looked away as Alastor cringed in searing pain that ran down his leg but he quickly regained his composure after taking a deep breath or two.

"I will create my own army." A big screen came down behind Alastor.

"I will control the dead, an army of mindless zombies. Ha, ha, yes the-"

Another young man in tank top and shorts runs inside and a frustrated Alastor screams out. "JOHNNY!!"

The young man was immediately escorted out and they returned their attention to the screen. The screen showed a group of zombies walking across a field, clumsily bumping into each other and Alastor continued but looked one last time toward the entrance to make sure he was not interrupted again. "Where was I?... Oh yes, world domination."

He proudly held up a small vial that almost bubbled over with neon green ooze. "I have the potion. Subject!"

Johnny the Weasel, a tall, dumb goon with wavy, ash hair and crooked nose, held a dead squirrel with tire tracks down its back.

"Is this what you brought me?" Alastor asked. Johnny the Weasel looked at him with slight confusion. "I thought you wanted a dead body?"

Johnny was a smalltime gangster from the East Coast who moved to Hollywood to become an extra for acting, mostly for the free food. He and Alastor met when Johnny was selling "Maps to the stars" and Johnny complained of the long hours.

Alastor slammed his fists on the table. "Body! ...Human!"

Johnny the Weasel sheepishly responded as he typically did.

"You, uh, didn't say human."

Alastor grabbed the squirrel from Johnny. "Just give me this." He held the squirrel close to his face as if preparing for delicate surgery and used a medicine dropper to insert the formula. He carefully put a drop onto the squirrel's tongue that hung to the side. All the men leaned close to watch. Alastor stood over his creation lying before him on the table, waiting in anticipation as his eyes became large.

A few seconds passed and nothing. "My solution is still unrefined." Alastor, a little embarrassed, admitted the failed experiment UNTIL- The squirrel coughed and then made a sudden jerking motion. His tiny legs convulsed for a moment. Triumphant, Alastor raised his fists toward the roof. "Life, my little friend, ***LIFE!!***"

Alastor turned to the scientist and nodded toward the squirrel.

"Check his vital signs."

"What?" The scientist gave Alastor an odd look when-

The squirrel jumped into Johnny the Weasel's hair. Johnny, screaming and grasping at his head, finally grabbed a hold of the squirrel and tossed it across the room as Alastor lunged toward it.

"Get that squirrel!"

Johnny the Weasel drew his pistol out of his belt and fired wild shots at the squirrel, taking out an expensive vase and putting a hole in the forehead of Alastor's portrait on the wall.

Alastor smacked him on the back of his head. "Not in the house, you idiot!"

Reece- a petite, cute girl in her early twenties and with a certain innocence, rushed through the room but Alastor was quick to cut her off. "Where are you going, my precious?"

She quickly tried to make her way around him. "Out!" She proclaimed.

Alastor firmly grabbed her hand, and then poked her finger with a small syringe but she desperately tried to pull away with no luck against his deceptive strength. "What are you doing?"

Alastor squeezed a couple of drops of blood into a vial. "Just checking your glucose." He tucked the vial away in his smoking jacket and tried to seduce her with his forked tongue and quivering lips.

"You're such a freak!" Aghast, she backed away clutching her finger. A smile crept across Alastor's face as he was quite proud of his new discovery. "You're so pure… Ohhh, so pure." His body trembled as he spoke and the men averted their attention elsewhere. Reece ran off toward the front door and out. Alastor turned to Johnny the Weasel, who was crawling under the table.

"Forget the squirrel, follow her." Alastor held the vial up. He shook it as a plume of green smoke rolled out the top.

THE LAST ASSIGNMENT

Hell, Somewhere buried in the Earth's Crust

The scene in Hades was not quite as festive. Shadows were thrown everywhere as fire blew a hundred feet up, barely touching craters, and a river of lava flowed below.

A winged creature drank from the river and then let out a shrill scream. Orco, still hung over and head aching, covered his ears.

"DO YOU MIND!?" He still wore his Mardi Gras beads and a t-shirt with "Show me your knockers!" on it. The winged creature slowly moved away from the river of fire. Its long, bony legs stepped back and then it opened its mouth revealing razor sharp teeth and spoke to him. "Shouldn't have been out all night." Orco mocked it back. "Shouldn't have been out all night."

He smacked the winged creature across the nose. "Hold that forked tongue of yours or I'll hold it for you!" The winged creature flew off over the river of fire. Orco rubbed his temples, and then growled as the other annoyed dark angels noticed. A two-headed dog barked and snarled at him causing a pleasant thought to reel through Orco's head. "Speakin' of hair of the dog."

Orco took a flask out and drank, a little dribble escaped down his chin. He tucked the flask away and then walked over to a group of good angels in white who stood in a line separate from the waiting dark angels.

Gabriel, the gatekeeper, and wearing a construction helmet, stepped in front of Orco. "Sorry, Orc. Gotta go back." Orco made his way around a line of plump cupids who sharpened their golden arrows.

"No need to apologize." He stretched his back and continued his conversation to himself. "Not sure for what... Me and the boys are done." Orco sipped on his flask again. "Time to be fitted for a new pair of wings. He slapped his robust belly. I'm trying to lose a few pounds. Really tough this time of-" This time, Gabriel was quick to cut him off. "One more before you get your wings."

Orco fumed with anger and then kneed a good angel in the groin and dropkicked a cupid across the river of fire. "No, that's bull!"

Gabriel went back to looking over the list as another good angel cautiously stepped forward and around Orco. Gabriel checked a name waving another angel through as he continued with Orco.

"You've taken way too many out before their prime, Orc."

A young kid on a ten speed bicycle peddled past them. "Yeah! I'm gonna be grounded for sure!"

"That will teach you to play in the street." Orco fired back.

The kid thumbed his nose at Orco. "Up yours!"

Orco reflected on the numerous mistakes and multiple deaths they had accidentally caused and turned to Gabriel to plead with him. "C'mon, Gabriel, the guys are packing. It's just not fair."

This did nothing for Gabriel as he waved a construction angel over who sat on a small, fluffy, artificial cloud brought over from heaven. Gabriel continued. "You think it's fair that we have to meet down here with you evil, no-good, worm infested--?"

Orco interrupted him, not needing a complete explanation. "It's not my fault you guys are always making improvements in Heaven." Orco's words were weak and whiny as he did not want to upset Gabriel, who for the moment held his destiny. Gabriel took his list and began to walk away.

"Just one more."

"How am I gonna explain it to the group? They thought they were getting their wings."

The construction angel moved next to Gabriel after finishing and waited for his next job. A visibly annoyed, shapely female harp player who didn't care about playing in Hell, plucked at the strings to drown out the wailing of misplaced souls who were buried up to their heads in the ground.

Disappointed, Orco stomped to the back of the line but turned around and walked back, cutting his way through the dark angel line. No was not an option. Not after all that they had been through. He was not going to give up on his team.

He was cut off by a sleazy, dark angel salesman in a polyester suit and holding a briefcase. "Hey, good buddy, you would look good in a 78 Lebaron. Or a 79 Cutlass-"

Orco shoved him aside and passed a gangster who relaxed a machine gun over his shoulder and a bald, overweight, profusely sweating Southern Alabama politician who constantly wiped his forehead.

The other line of pristine angels in white pointed and laughed at the dark angels.

The politician leaned forward and peered around the line. "How long is this gonna take? I mean maybe we could allot times and-" The salesman whipped out his business card and tucked it in his pocket.

"Just like you politicians. Always wanting a deal."

"Who said anything about a deal?" The politician responded as he checked his watch, which had evidently stopped, judging by his tapping on it. The salesman winked at the politician and sounded off in a vibrant tone.

"Then how about a Chevy at ten percent off?!"

Sal, a dignified, elderly angel with white but graying wings around the edges, chuckled to himself as Orco stepped forward.

"You dark angels are always so theatrical."

Sal slid in front of Orco as they took their scrolls off a table piled high with others. Sal carefully looked his scroll over. "A tandem, huh?"

This was unique for Sal, but he was willing to make an exception for his last assignment and take on two. He had always gone above and beyond what was always asked of him, much like his job as a gritty fireman in Chicago back in the early forties. He made a career out of saving people's lives. Maybe going out with a bang wasn't so bad.

Orco disappointingly looked toward Gabriel who stopped him from opening his scroll.

"Who is it this time?" Orco complained.

"Just open it when you get to wherever your--" Orco ripped open the scroll. "I know you, Gabriel, and the only time you don't want me to see it-- Hey, wait!"

A dark angel lawyer nudged closer to Orco. "I'd sue if I were you." Gabriel and Orco both barked at the lawyer. "Back in line!" The lawyer winked and slipped something to Orco. "Here's my card."

"This means a real bad assignment." Orco thought out loud as he pointed at the gangster who had a cigarette hanging out of the lower corner of his mouth. "How about him?"

The gangster responded with the cigarette bobbing up and down. "Hey, pretty boy, I don't keep taking them out before their prime." Orco leaned close to Gabriel. "Does everyone know about this?"

"You guys are sort of the talk around here." Gabriel admitted.

An angel gambler standing next to a board with Orco's name at the top, pointed at it as other angels threw their money at him.

"Taking all bets!"

Orco grumbled to himself as numbers on the board soared higher and angels tried to cash in on the Death Squad's incompetence.

Gabriel offered Sal, who had been waiting patiently, a solid handshake. "Congrats, Sal, you've earned retirement." Sal received a few pats on the wing as he proudly waved his scroll in the air further angering a jealous Orco. He looked back at Orco with a sly grin and the good angels cheered for him. A trumpet sounded off and the trumpeter angel who was joining the harp player, apologized for the loud outburst while warming up to play.

Sal boasted as he spoke to nobody in particular. "No more pulling mortals out of burning buildings, steering the car when they fall asleep, or saving women from evil men. What am I gonna do with my time?"

"Breaks my heart." Orco mocked as he felt like a disappointment to the team and Sal laughed at his predicament. "Bet it does… Looking forward to my time off in heaven."

Orco moved forward and tried to shove Sal aside but neither stubborn angel budged. "Do you mind?" Orco asked.

Orco flexed his broad, black wings and snapped Sal in the face. Sal hit him back with the back of his hand and they dropped their scrolls and grabbed each other's throats while their wings flapped wildly. Gabriel broke them up as the numbers on the board soared even higher. Glaring at each other, they reached down to pick up the scrolls. Sal mumbled under his breath. "Rookie."

Orco muttered back. "Fossil."

Gabriel shoved them apart. "This might be your last assignment but you're still on a time frame." Gabriel continued to Orco. "And Orco…"

The angel gambler could be seen in the background with other angels crowding around and frantically waving money.

"One million to one!" The angel gambler announced as Orco yelled back at him with disbelief. "One million to one? Oh, come on!! We're better than that!"

Gabriel gave Orco a stern look and finished. "Be careful."

They went their separate ways with each other's assignment as the trumpet player laid his horn at his side and snapped his fingers.

"Let's get this party started! A one, two, a, one, two, three, four…"

SAL AND GUS

Sky (as in high above), New Mexico

An airplane sliced through a cloud over Eastern New Mexico toward Sacramento. Sal sat on the wing of the airplane and smoked a plump cigar while clutching the wing of the plane with the other hand. He relished the thought of retirement as he flipped open a travel brochure of Heaven that revealed glistening castles, houses and domes that were splashed on the cover. He winked at a gawking child peering out at him and the brochure flew out of his hand and fluttered away into the sky. The child waved and Sal playfully made a face back and then waved back with his free hand.

A crow landed on the wing with a small note in its claw. Sal took the note and read it. He tossed it aside and grabbed the scroll out of his pocket, quickly unrolling it to see if it was true. "Alastor" was listed at the top in bold, black letters. Sal threw his hands up in a panic and was immediately swept off of the wing, sending him spiraling out of control to earth below.

He first bounced off of a smiling, sunflower hot air balloon and flipped erratically through the air. He did his best to flap his wings and gain control mid-air before he crash-landed when he spotted a stack of hay to land on and did his best to aim for it.

Down below on an old farmhouse porch, Gus Babcock, an aging, leathery farmer in dirty overalls, took a long swig off a half-empty liquor bottle and cradled his shotgun in his lap. Sal waved both arms at him.

"Prepare for landing!"

Sal torpedoed through the air until- THUMP! He straddled the farmhouse roof instead, missing his target by a few feet and desperately reaching forward for the rooster weather vane. Gus dropped his bottle and instinctively reached for his shotgun. Without batting an eye, he aimed high. BOOM! Sal was shot and blown off the roof. An explosion of feathers slowly made its way to the ground. Gus crept around with rifle pointed to see what he had hit.

Sal, dazed and still holding his groin, moaned and looked up at a small shed where a dead alien with a huge gunshot hole in its chest, sat propped up. Sal's expression was one of pain and disorientation as he uncoiled on the ground and laid flat on his wings that had little life in them. He looked up to see Gus standing over him and told Gus in a high pitch voice, "Please stay seated until the seat belt light goes off and thank you for flying the friendly skies with us."

Sal passed out from the pain as his wing smoked. Gus let out a sigh and then threw the aging angel over his shoulder.

The crow, holding another message in its claws, watched from a roof top and decided to fly off.

REID AND REECE

Los Angeles, California

It was a nice, sunny day in Los Angeles with its usual healthy haze of brownish, yellow smog in the air.

Reece rushed into a record store looking over her shoulder the entire time and Reid Wallace, tall, athletic and twenty six, did inventory on the "Jazz" rack for the store he managed during the day. He looked down at an inventory sheet and scribbled some numbers and then strolled over to another rack and flipped through some albums when his hand hit another soft, delicate hand.

"Excuse-"

She abruptly pulled away but took a long look into his eyes as if meeting at that moment was planned by a higher authority. She spoke softly with a little hesitation. "I'm sorry." Reid didn't want to lose this moment so he picked up the album she was reaching for and assisted her.

"So, you like jazz?"

Johnny the Weasel, doing his best to be incognito, watched quietly from another section as a child tried to grab an album high above him and then began to whimper when he came up far short. Johnny, not taking his eyes off Reece, leaned down and whispered to the child. "This never happened." He picked the child up, partially using him as a shield as he spied on Reece. Knowing that Johnny was always close by, she broke away from Reid. "I've got to go."

Johnny the Weasel, in a rush to keep her in his sight, placed and left the small child on the top rack. He shuffled down the aisle crouching and grabbing albums to conceal his identity, though he was not fooling anyone, including the other annoyed customers who scrambled to get out of his way. Reid grabbed at her hand but she was already backing away toward the exit. Johnny the Weasel followed but looked back at the child and winked. "Thanks for giving me cover." He ran around a rack and toward the glass front door, slamming face first against it and then out as he followed Reece.

Benny, short nerdy type in his mid-twenties and Reid's best friend, ran up to Reid. "That was Al's girl." Benny grew up in

Hollywood and always made it his business to know who was new to the neighborhood as he delivered their newspapers.

"Al?" Reid obviously had no idea who Benny was even talking about and watched the door, hoping she was not gone forever.

"The big spaghetti!" Benny, overly agitated and nervous as usual, told him. "His wife?" Reid asked.

"Not his wife. That's some old bag that has her nails done in Europe. That's his girl," Benny warned.

Reid watched a red Porsche drive away and a long black Cadillac followed closely behind. He pulled his keys out of his pocket and made his way to his dinged up, rusted car, which was parked in front of the door. "I have to follow her."

"You've got a death wish." Benny warned but Reid was already out the door.

Deep down under the earth's surface, Orco laid on the hood of his car smoking a cigarette and listening to classical music so he could clear his head. He pondered his situation and how he would explain it to the rest of the group. He knew that, despite Pierrot's rugged appearance, she had been known to check herself in a mirror and freshen up with a little makeup. Perneum would dive into clouds pretending they were the tall grass he used to dive into as a young child in the English countryside. Artesia had tried on a white robe or two and Orco himself, would just like to be one of the good guys for a change.

The pleasant thought was soon interrupted when a boulder rumbled up above, and after tumbling down, bounced off of his head. A dazed Orco rolled off of the hood and pulled out his keys made of genuine shin bone.

The engine roared as he fired up the Death Mobile and the gargoyle hood ornament wore an excavator's hat. Fire blew out of the back and the Death Mobile was once again off through the earth's crust with Orco at the wheel.

Back at the farmhouse, Gus handed Sal a shot of whiskey. Sal's eyes were glossy and darted around the room with a look of bewilderment, as he finally came to his senses… But, in a state of agitation. "THEY TOOK THE WRONG ONE! THEY TOOK THE WRONG ONE!" Sal slammed the shot of whiskey, then grabbed the bottle and took a long swig. Gus took the bottle from him and put it on the table. "You're an angel sent for-?"
Sal swiped the bottle from his hand. "Here I land in God-knows-where and you shoot me. You know you're a real jerk!"

"Maybe you shouldn't drink anymore." Gus suggested as Sal taunted him with the bottle, and then crashed it over his head, knocking him out cold. "That's for shooting me." Sal grabbed a set of truck keys from Gus' overall pocket. "See ya in about ten years." He was out the door and headed toward California.

DISSENSION IN THE GROUP

Perneum walked back to the group using the skeletal remains of an arm as a back scratcher and then snapped it in half in a rage. Artesia threw his hands up. "Who keeps making the mistake?" He winced when he touched the infected and damaged wing and Pierrot slapped the hood of the Death Mobile. It growled back at her and blew a tiny stream of black smoke from under its hood.

Orco tried to calm the group down as best as he could with flattery. "I think it was an assignment they needed the experts on." He noticed a slimy goo coming out of Artesia's wing. "You should do something for that wing."

"What's it really matter?" a frustrated Artesia told him. He plopped down in a wooden coffin for a short nap.

Pierrot offered up her not so cheerful opinion. "Just not meant to be. We were scum in life and we'll be scum in the afterlife." They all found this hard to argue as Artesia sat up and glared toward Perneum. "Who keeps knocking people off?"

"Why are you looking at me?" Perneum looked over at Orco for any assistance and Artesia persisted in pointing the blame at the one he's always suspected. "I don't know, Perneum, why am I? Planning wars, natural disasters… Why would I be looking at his unholiness' most trusted assistant?"

"That was a long time ago!" Perneum fired back and Artesia got to his feet and towered over him. Orco quickly shoved him away.

"We're a team, so knock it off!" Orco paused. "One big one and a few small ones that are totally optional." Orco acted as if they were no big deal.

"We can handle one more assignment." Pierrot told them while sharpening a large knife on a granite tombstone. "**One** more." She reiterated, glaring at Orco.

"I didn't like you guys at first but I'm okay with one more assignment," Perneum announced as he continued leering in Artesia's direction. "Most of you guys."

A crow with a wad of paper in its claw, "kaaaa'd" above them and Perneum spat at it but missed and the spit continued off deep into space.

Orco laughed and tried to lift their spirits to keep the group from losing faith. "One more poor soul, guys. That's it. Piece of cake... Nothing to it." Artesia grumbled, having heard this many times before but Orco slapped him on the shoulder. "Come on, Art." Orco pulled out a rope from his jacket. "We'll hang em'. That is your favorite isn't it, Art?"

Perneum, hanging his head, held his hand up. "Mine."

"That's right, it's yours Perneum." Orco thought about it and then pulled out a large sledge hammer. "Am I almost there?"

Pierrot raised her hand but Artesia reluctantly broke into a half smile and Orco considered his little pep talk a raging success. "That's what I like to see!!"

Artesia sat on a tombstone. "I'm okay." He extended a handshake to Perneum. "Sorry, Troll."

Perneum, who always held a grudge, was not so quick to forgive and gave him an evil eye before walking away. Artesia whined to Orco.

"What? I apologized, didn't I?"

"Close enough." Quipped Orco, still struggling to keep the mood upbeat. "What is your favorite death, Art?"

Artesia pretended to be sullen as he looked at the ground. "I detest death, Orco." The guys looked up this time as Artesia did his best to conceal his laughter. "Just kidding! Who's our next victim?"

Orco went for the list. The crow "kaaa'd" again, desperately trying to get their attention as it clung to a tiny message in its claws and Orco blew fire at it. SPLAT! Bird poop ran down the scroll that was laid out on the hood of the Death Mobile. Orco angrily waved his finger at the bird and walked to the Death Mobile as the crow "kaaa'd" again. SPLAT! It crapped on the car.

Orco, enraged, opened his mouth and his long tongue snatched up the crow and zipped it back in his watering mouth. Feathers flew as Orco belched and thumped his belly with his fist because of the usual indigestion.

The paper still attached to claws, dropped to the ground as Orco went back to the scroll. He studied it with difficulty. "The lucky guys are-- Hmmm? I thought there was one name?" Orco turned it sideways and then around as Perneum ran to him. "Can you make out that word?" Orco asked Perneum. Artesia rolled his eyes and went back to the coffin. "Here we go again."

"I'm sure they keep copies at-" Pierrot suggested but was quickly cut off by Orco, who rarely followed directions and always did things his own way. "No! No way. We'll figure it out. Just might need a little help. C'mon, let's go."

The foursome piled into the Death Mobile and took their spots. Artesia, sitting in the back, offered a suggestion. "Perneum is pretty tight with the guys downstairs, maybe he can-" THWANG! A knife stuck in Artesia's forehead. Perneum wiped off his hands from the passenger front seat.

"That was a long time ago."

Artesia looked up and pointd at his forehead with the knife protruding from it. "Orco! The dwarf just stabbed me!"

Orco pulled out his keys, not much in the mood for their petty fighting and fired up the Death Mobile. It rumbled and blew out flames as the gargoyle hood ornament wore a tiny Viking helmet with a clear protective shield. Orco threw it in gear. "You boys break it up. We have work to do."

THE SEARCH FOR R. WALLACE

South Central Los Angeles, California

Pervis, a wiry twenty-seven-year-old black man with a shady past of petty crimes, wore a panty hose that hung loosely over his narrow face. He pointed a gun at the Indian man behind the counter who showed little expression. "How about that bottle of Scotch?" Pervis demanded.

The stone-faced Indian employee looked Pervis up and down.

"Not old enough." Pervis couldn't believe this and waved his gun in front of him.

"You're being held up." The Indian man nodded his head with disapproval. "Need to see I.D." Pervis threw up his arms and couldn't believe all of this trouble, though for him it was very typical. "I.D??" The Indian man still didn't budge. "Yes. I.D.,Sir." Pervis pulled out his driver's license and the employee looked it over, then gladly put the bottle in the bag. Smiling,"You do nice work. Come again, my friend."

Pervis walked out of the store with a cocky swagger and bobbed his head from side to side. "It's about time I got the respect I deserve." Inside the mart, the Indian man punched numbers on the phone and calmly spoke into it. "Pervis Gentry... 4455 Sycamore." Close by, the Death Mobile cruised slowly down the dark street when Pervis cut them off, holding out the gun. He slapped the hood and the gargoyle hood ornament bit at his hand. "Outta the car!" Pervis demanded as he moved swiftly around to Orco's side window. Orco, unfazed, if not somewhat amused, still tried to make out the writing on the scroll but struggled. "You don't know a Re—Re--?"

Pervis waved the gun. "Do I look like I know a Re, Re--?" Orco looked up from the scroll. "Last name Wallace?" "I think I just told you to evacuate the car, mother--!" CRUNCH!

Pervis jumped away from the car as the gargoyle on the hubcap had just bitten him. He rubbed his ankle. Orco turned to Perneum. "Grab the list," and then to Pervis, "We'll give you anything you want as long as we know your name." Police cars screamed by them with lights on and Pervis tucked his gun into his baggy pants as he began to sweat. This was all becoming too much.

"Okay. Sixth... Sense. Yeah, I'm the Sixth Sense."

"Check it." Orco told Perneum and then to the back. "Okay, pony up. If you're gonna make up a name, Sixth Sense is a right good one." They all nodded in compliance. Orco pulled out his lighter with a small pewter skull on the side that hissed at Pervis. He fired up the cigarette and took a long drag. "You heard the man."

"The man. Yeah, that's right."

They all reached into their pockets and handed him skulls, snakes, fingers, and eyeballs. Sweat began to collect on his forehead as Pervis was now shaking and no longer enjoying this.

"You are a bunch of crazy mothers. Just give me the car!" He looked up, as he could hear more police sirens growing closer.

Orco calmly puffed on the cigarette and exhaled a little waft of smoke which formed a skull and crossbones in front of Pervis. Pervis shook the gun at them, then took a drink of Scotch and handed the bottle to the guys, who gladly passed it around. "I want this car right-" BOOM! The gun fired off.

The dark angels looked around and nobody seemed to be harmed until they realized Artesia's chest was smoking with a bullet hole in the middle. Artesia touched it and then looked over at Pervis. "The hell was that for!?" Orco stepped out, tossed down his cigarette and stomped it out. "I'm done fooling around. What's your name!?" Pervis studied the frightening group. "Pervis Ggggentry." Perneum took an eyeglass out and looked closer at the list. "Not getting any Gggggen-- Wait a minute. Hmmm?" Pervis stared at the gun and then started to move away from the car. "I thought it was a starter pistol."

Pervis ran down the neighborhood street to his house nearby.

"You can't run from death!" Orco warned. Pervis, already out of breath, stopped at a house when he saw it was surrounded by police. "This can't be happening." He turned and was surprised to see Orco standing next to him. Pervis trembled as he held out a small pocketknife. Orco picked at his teeth with a large knife and then checked his fingernails. "Remember me?"

The police shined their flashlights in their direction. Orco knew he had him where he wanted him. "Seems you need our help now."

Pervis dropped to his knees and sobbed. “Don’t hurt me… Please.” Pervis was jerked up to his feet and ushered back to the Death Mobile.

He sat in the back between Pierrot and Artesia. “I don’t know any R-... What did you call him?” Orco returned his attention to the scroll in his hand. “He resides at Sycamore--”

“Sycamore runs all the way through Los Angeles. Is it street, place, court, avenue--?”

“Just help us find him.”

Orco handed the scroll back to Perneum as Pervis leaned forward. “You know where you’re at? You know how many people live in this city?”

They all looked at each other with no idea and Pervis continued.

“You guys like bounty hunters or somethin’?”

“Something like that.” Artesia told him.

Pervis checked the scroll over front and back. “Is that bird poop?”

They grumbled and Perneum tapped on the scroll as Orco swiped it from him. “What about Hollywood?” Pervis broke out in nervous laughter. “You’re looking for Hollywood?” He quickly continued,

“You took a wrong turn at Crenshaw,” then paused briefly.

“Speaking of which, there are probably some brothers taking your hubcaps as we speak.”

The hubcaps had already clamped down on a couple of thugs who tried to steal them but the thieves were now on their knees and struggling to break free. This didn’t help Pervis at all, who was pulling for the thugs, or at least a distraction. Orco looked at Pervis in the rear view mirror.

“Consider yourself in good hands as long as you help us.” Pervis was not exactly relieved as Orco turned the ignition and bolts of lightning screamed out the back. “I don’t usually go with strangers but I’ll make an exception.” Pervis slapped at Perneum’s list. “Put that thing away.” Pervis looked up as jagged spikes made their way up the side windows. Pierrot glanced over at Pervis.

“Child proof.” She told him much to his dismay and Perneum painted a small skull and crossbones on the scroll.

The Death Mobile traveled down the street in a gang ridden

section of Los Angeles and then pulled over into the parking lot of a run-down gas station tattooed with graffiti. Orco was the first one out, quickly followed by Pervis, who crawled over Artesia.

Pervis flipped through the white pages at a phone booth when a group of Latino gang bangers strolled up and flipped various gang signs to an unimpressed Orco. One Latino moved close to Orco, trying to get a reaction. "I think you're in the wrong neighborhood, Esse,"

Orco swatted him away with his large forearm. "Beat it, Fly Boy!"

Orco took the phone book from Pervis and the insulted street thug looked back at his "homeboys". He thumped Orco on the back. "Hey, we're talking to you, Stinky Amigo."

Orco was still looking for the name and didn't have time for this. "I said--!" Orco's eyes lit up fire-red as he grabbed his arm, etching his fingernail into the homeboy's tattoo of Satan. Smoke rose from his arm as he fought to pull it away. "What are you doing, bro?" The others watched in horror as Orco abruptly let go, stood back, and admired his work. The tattoo now said, "Orco was here" with a sketch of a chainsaw wielding madman next to it. The homeboy ran off screaming with his gang close behind him. "Loco!"

Orco went back to flipping through the yellow pages when Pervis held out a page he ripped out. "You're lucky. There are only five Reid Wallaces and eighteen R. Wallaces in the LA area." Orco tossed aside the phone book. "Let's get started on them."

The guys stood outside the window frame in a middle class residential neighborhood and peered into a room where a small boy in rocket ship pajamas slept.

"Ya think?" Orco asked them and Pervis cringed.

"Just a little kid."

Perneum had already begun to crawl through the window with a knife in his mouth. "I'll do it."

Orco pulled him off. "You notch another accidental and you'll be smoking turds in hell for an eternity."

Orco waved them on as he almost tripped on a sprinkler on his way back to the car. "Let's check out a few more." They walked side by side in the middle of a football field when a Junior in high school with Wallace on the back of his jersey stopped in front of them cradling the football and the opposing team close behind him.

"Do you mind, I'm trying to score?"

Orco held out his arm, blocking him. "Are you Reid Wallace?"

"Who?"

He was quickly tackled and piled on under the bright lights of the small stadium.

Disappointed, Pierrot looked over at Orco as Pervis was talking to the cheerleaders. "I think we have the wrong guy. Artesia started walking back. "Let's hit a couple more." The guys snuck off the field as players carried off the ailing football player.

An older man, Reid "Ford" Wallace, ran on the treadmill at a health spa. He turned off his Ipod and took off his headphones as Orco stood next to him. "Do you live on Sycamore? Any relation to the evil dead?"

"I sell insurance." He told them huffing and puffing as sweat dripped from his chin. Perneum pulled out a large knife. "Close enough." The guys stood behind him holding weapons except for Artesia who had his head stuck in a weight machine. Orco studied the man for a moment with a tinge of doubt. "We might have the wrong guy." Perneum edged even closer with his knife out. "I think he's a liar." A bubbly blonde eagerly ran up to them. "Like to join?" Pierrot sneered at her appearance. Frustrated, they dropped their weapons to their side and filed out the front door.

The group, defeated, walked down the street past a wooden telephone pole littered with fliers and Pervis pulled one off. "I have a clue, but it will cost you." It was quickly jerked out of his hand and Orco shoved it in his pocket.

Orco and the guys were grouped around a sorority girl as she stood in front of the sorority house in her flowery pajamas. He held up the flier.

"You girls have a Reid Wallace playing your party." The stuck-up sorority girl flipped up her hair as she stood behind the door.

"That was last night, a-hole."

"But-" Orco tried to continue as he received odd glares from other girls who joined her in the doorway and another sorority girl smacked loudly on her gum. "It's against the rules to see boys after ten. Our boyfriends would kick your ass."

Stella, a shy, gothic-looking girl with long, jet black hair, leaned out a second floor window watching the group. She admired Artesia. "Hi."

The sorority girl continued with her nose in the air. "Take her. She looks weird enough for you freaks." Two girls looked at each other and laughed as they said in unison. "Legacy."

"I think he's playing another party tomorrow night." Stella told Artesia.

Meanwhile at the mansion, Johnny the Weasel walked to the front door when Alastor's voice blared out of an intercom. "Did you wash your hands?" Johnny the Weasel looked around to see if anyone was watching.

"Yes."

"Bull Monkey! Get back and wash your hands!!" broadcasted through the speaker on the wall and Johnny the Weasel rolled his eyes. Alastor continued. "Hurry up! I have a mission for you." Johnny the Weasel rushed to the bathroom, turned on the hot water, and muttered to himself. "So anal."

"I heard that!"

Johnny the Weasel gave up on looking for the speaker and grabbed the soap and scrubbed as he finished his thought.

"Analytical. You're so analytical."

Johnny the Weasel dried off his hands and rushed out. He was almost out the front door when Alastor called out to him. "You wanna know your mission or are you just gonna walk out of here like an uncaged idiot?"

Weasel stopped and turned, looking for the hidden speaker.

"Oh, yeah, to the mission part."

"Take some boys over to the nuclear plant." Alastor told him.

Johnny the Weasel looked under plants, at the wall, at his palm, confusedly searching for whichever speaker was broadcasting Alastor's voice when he was hit on the head with a gray ceramic planter from above, sending him crashing to the ground. "Up here, you jackass!"

Alastor looked down from the second story landing and tossed him the keys. Johnny the Weasel gave him a blank stare as he got to his feet.

"Go now!" Alastor demanded.

The truck pulled up to the nuclear plant and parked in a dark corner of the parking lot. Johnny the Weasel hopped out and ran toward the building, making sure he wasn't spotted and disappeared inside a white building. A few minutes passed and he exited back out of the building and waved "bye" at a plant worker who counted out some money in his hand. A couple of goons backed up the truck.

Johnny trotted back holding the container of nuclear waste and complained about Alastor. "He can't boss me around like that." A goon put on protective gloves and reached forward with a protective container.

"What are you talking about, Weasel?"

Johnny the Weasel handed him a container and then held up a small vial of green gloop. "I grabbed a little of the solution for myself… Ya know they produce that stuff next to the cafeteria?" Johnny took a little nuclear waste and poured it into the solution and took off his gloves. "Gonna show him..." He shook it up and then swirled it. The goon pointed. "Uh, Weasel?" Johnny the Weasel took off his gloves. "Did I say you could refer to me as Weasel?" The goon pointed as the solution bubbled over Johnny's finger. Johnny put the lid back on. "See. That's all there is-" Johnny's finger glowed and seemed to take on a life of its own. It poked him in the eye. The goon's head dropped. "We're in trouble."

THE LONG TRIP

Highway, Northern Arizona

On a long stretch of road with nothing in sight but surrounding mountains in the distance and dry cracked desert, Sal stood stranded on the side of the road beside the truck as a crow flew away. He looked up as a car swerved back and forth, rapidly heading his direction. Sal hunched down and looked closer to see that the driver was asleep as the car barreled forward. He stretched his legs and shoulders out as he did a couple of forward lunges to loosen up and prepare himself for the worst.

"Why?" He asked himself as he jumped in the middle of the road waving his arms and wings. "Hey! Hey!" BOOM!

Feathers flew as Sal went sailing over the hood and bouncing off the roof before landing in the middle of the road.

The driver abruptly woke up and controlled the steering. He looked back wide-eyed, not sure of what he hit.

Sal picked himself up and dusted himself off. "You're welcome!" Sal screamed. "Never again," he told himself until he noticed a nearby house that went up in flames. Sal rolled his eyes again, wondering how his luck could be so bad.

A woman ran out of the house screaming for help. He walked over a field toward the house as one wing was bent behind him. "I'm gonna kill Orco." He looked toward the sky. "Who's on call?!" Sal flapped his wings and took off for the house.

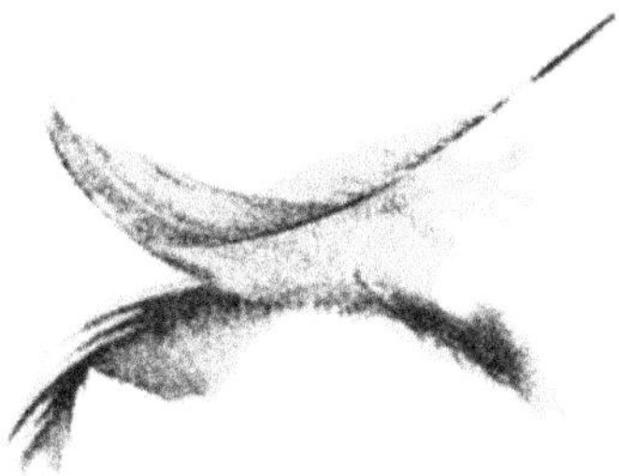

THE INVITE

Nearby, Reid put up fliers and watched the red Porsche pass by with Reece driving it. He quickly jumped in his car and backed out, almost hitting another car in the parking lot. Reid pulled forward and sped out onto the street, struggling to catch up. She turned and he was right behind her, destined to catch up.

Reece blew through a stop sign in a residential neighborhood and Reid turned in behind her, wheels screeching. She finally slowed and pulled into the entrance of the mansion but Reid drove over the grass and cut her off. He hopped out and stood in front of her car with both hands on the hood. "I'm not moving until you give me your name."

"You shouldn't have followed me here."

Reece watched the gate open and kept an eye out for Johnny the Weasel who was also struggling to keep up. Reid ran around the car to her window holding a flier and a music CD. "I'm DJ'ing a party for a bunch of frat boys tomorrow night. I would like to see you." He slid the CD and flier through the window but the window rolled up and caught his sleeve as the car rolled forward. Reid ran with the car as he struggled to keep his footing until he dropped the flyers. "Hey! Stop!" The dark tinted window inched down and Reid rolled to the side as the Porche disappeared down the cobblestone driveway.

Reid rolled into the bushes as the black Cadillac drove behind them and stopped. Johnny the Weasel leaned out and grabbed a flier. He slapped at it, proud of his find, and tucked it in his pocket. He pulled up through the driveway and Reid raced back to his car.

The Death Mobile, finally out of traffic, continued along the street as Pervis, sitting in the back of the car, spoke out to the group.

"If I help find this guy then you dudes gotta help me." They found this mildly amusing and Pervis slunk back in his seat, squashed between Pierrot and Artesia.

"How about we don't add you to our list?" Orco offered. Perneum, still looking over the list, ran his fingers along it and stopped.

"Stop. Pervis Gen-" Pervis pointed out the front window. "It's Medusa in a bikini!" Perneum glanced up and Pervis swiped his list and tossed it out the window. "Must have been a tourist." Pervis told them as Perneum looked at another list and quickly pointed out the window.

Orco changed lanes. "Got a lively one, eh?"

They parked in front of a restaurant patio on the Hollywood strip. The smell of freshly baked bread and Italian cuisine filled the air as the group exited the car and made their way to the small tables that sat out under the California sunshine.

Max Sloan, tanned action star with a square jaw, and his date, a young, vivacious brunette, sat at an outdoor dining table as the Death Squad sauntered up to them. Max glanced up from his menu and flashed his million dollar smile. "Can I help you, gents?" He winked at Pierrot. "And, uh, Pretty lady?"

"Are you Max Sloan, the action star?" asked Perneum. Max winked at Perneum and smiled at his date. "Look. I'll be signing autographs tomorrow but you're making the lady a little nervous." Artesia sipped on Max's cocktail as it splashed out of the hole in his chest and down the front of his black robe.

Perneum grinned at Max. "You were great in "Slayers of Paradiso" but you know you should have died when you did a swan dive into the fire pit of hell." Max chuckled at this statement and tossed his napkin on the table.

"That was just a movie, little buddy. I have a stunt double. Think I would do anything to damage this million dollar face?" Max gathered up his keys and grabbed his jacket. Orco pulled out a large axe from his jacket as Artesia put on rubber gloves. A security guard lunged forward but Orco cupped his head and the guard dropped to his knees and started crying. Max was equally distraught as he began to plead, "Who are you people!?"

Orco positioned himself by the exit of the patio and called out to Perneum. "You sure he's on the list, 'cause you know we've already got fourteen strikes against us?" Perneum read off the list again just to make sure. "He's got syphilis and all the drugs should have caused cardiac arrest many times." The young brunette tossed her menu aside and scooted away. Max was getting mad now.

"List!? List? Syphilis?! Drugs? Did the tabloids link that!? I'll sue."

Perneum looked back at the list and nodded his head. "I checked it twice. He's due."

Orco faced the other customers. "You folks might want to turn your heads."

Pierrot stopped Orco and pointed at the back alley as Max resisted.

"Wanna ride around in my car? Hell, take my car. Here's the keys."

They yanked Max away from the table and dragged him to the back alley. "But, I'm an action hero!"

Winona, Arizona

Sal, banged up and burned, checked his pockets as he pulled into an old gas station and found a little change when the dirty attendant walked out wiping his hands on an oilstained towel.

The attendant spit tobacco in the dirt, allowing a little to dribble down the side of his cheek. "Pay inside." Sal checked his pockets and unfortunately came up with nothing. "I have a little problem." The attendant tucked his grimy towel into his dirty overalls. "What would that be, pops? No cash?"

"You don't understand. I'm responsible for saving a life." Sal told him, but the greasy attendant was already looking over the old truck. "I get that a lot, old man. It's still cash up front." Sal smiled and winked, trying to persuade him. "What if I told you I could put in a good word with the guy upstairs? Get you a nice place, maybe something with a view." The attendant just stared at Sal with his mouth wide open and Sal gave up, frustrated. "Fine."

Sal started walking away and the attendant dropped his head and began to feel a little sentimental for the old angel… Just a little.

"Awww shucks, hold on..."

Sal eagerly turned around and the attendant nodded toward an old bike leaning against the station. "Take this old bicycle… least I can do."

A well-endowed blonde in a bikini dipped her toe in the water at Alastor's mansion when Johnny the Weasel walked by and knocked her in with a subtle shove to the back. He laughed to himself and then roamed to a table where Alastor sat and sipped on an expensive wine. Johnny the Weasel proudly handed Alastor the flier. "The guy gave her this." Alastor looked it over. "Frat party, huh?"

"I think he likes her." Alastor stared at Johnny the Weasel with disbelief. "No kidding, Numbnuts."

"Why do you have to call me names?" Johnny sheepishly complained.

Alastor tossed the paper aside. "I'm gonna tell you something wiseguy, bonehead, moron, jackass, dirtbag."

Johnny the Weasel straightened up and took a deep breath like a scorned school boy and knew he couldn't win. "I'm listening."

"Where I come from, if you can't handle it, you hit the road, or the skies, so, if this is too much for you-"

"I can handle it." Weasel told him with little confidence but not wanting Alastor to continue with the insults.

"Good. Now I want you to follow her." Alastor rubbed his head as his hair slid a little to the side. Johnny the Weasel gave him a funny look and then pointed. "Uh, Al?" Alastor slapped his cane down.

"Didn't I just give you a mission?"

"But your-" Johnny the Weasel couldn't help himself as he leaned close and reached out to Alastor's forehead but Alastor swatted at him. "GO!!" Johnny the Weasel ran off as a small horn protruded from Alastor's head.

SAL AND GUS REUNITE

An old sign about to tumble to the ground, dotted with bullet holes, read "California 78 miles."

The rickety old bike traveled down the middle of the highway. Sal tapped on a small transistor radio strapped to the handle bar with rusty wire. Distorted Mexican music played, then country, and then an alien talk show that cut in and out. A man called into the radio station and talked in a gravelly voice with a twang. "Winged creatures fly amongst us all the time. They read our minds! They study us like mice."

"How (distorted) know all this?" The radio host asked the mysterious caller.

Unbeknownst to Sal, an old motorcycle came flying over the hill in the distance with Gus hunched forward wearing large round goggles and intently staring ahead. The motorcycle bounced a couple of times sending Gus, bouncing off the seat but still fiercely gripping the handle bars.

The caller on the radio continued. "I know this, because… from the planet, Zodon."

"Uranus, more like it." Sal mumbled to himself with a chuckle.

Sal looked back at the approaching bike and his legs churned faster and wings flapped harder.

Gus adjusted his goggles and quickly caught up to Sal, who pulled off of the main highway and onto a dirt road.

"What happened to my truck!?" Gus screamed as he reached over with his hand and hooked Sal's mouth to stop him but Sal bit back.

"OWWWWWW! I'll kill you!"

"You've already tried and failed!" Sal peddled faster but Gus grabbed Sal's injured wing. "Damn you!" Sal stuck his finger in Gus' eye and Gus cried out. "Aaaarrrggggghhhh!" Gus grabbed his hand and bit it as Sal fought him off. "I damn you to hell!"

They both tumbled as the bikes collided, sending the motorcycle and bicycle sliding in the dirt off of the road and Sal and Gus rolling in the dirt and gravel. Sal jumped up and ran as Gus chased him, and then tackled him. Dust flew up as they threw vicious punches into each other.

HALLOWEEN FRAT PARTY

The ghouls were out in Hollywood for Halloween, not that Halloween made much of a difference in Hollywood. Orco wore a leather jacket and greased-back his hair as Artesia was an Indian with a bead in the middle of his head to cover the bullet hole. Perneum was dressed as a pirate, complete with eye patch, Pierrot decided on going out as a Catholic school girl and Pervis went as a cowboy. Orco felt the lining in his jacket. "I love Halloween." Perneum looked him over from top to bottom. "You didn't even dress up… You always wear that."

Pervis was starting to loosen up and studied the group with mild approval. "Let's get our swerve on."

Perneum pouted, "Still wish I could've been a Ninja." He trudged forward with the group.

Young people in costumes rushed around to set up the party in a fraternity house dining room that had the tables stacked in the corner.

Reid set up his music on a table with the help of Benny.

"Keep an eye out for her." Reid told him and then continued, "and those thugs who followed her here."

Benny stood high on the stage and looked out over the crowd. A frat boy lit a Tiki torch but dropped the lighter fluid on the tile floor and wiped it up with a paper towel. He turned to another. "Where is the garbage, bro?"

"Uh, just flush it down the toilet," the other one mentioned. He walked to the bathroom and tossed the towel in the toilet and went back looking for his beer.

Orco and the group approached the open front door with Pervis, who was busy checking out the women and liked what he saw, judging by his toothy smile. Frat boys dressed as ghosts and skeletons, passed them as they walked inside and a panicked Artesia grabbed a young man dressed as the Devil. "Did Lucifer send you!?"

The frat boy looked Artesia over, not sure of what to think of his costume. "Is he running the keg? Yeah..."

Pervis was worried that the guys were blowing their cover and quietly tried to get their attention. He put his hand up for Artesia to simmer down but they had no idea what he meant.

"WE ARE TOO LATE!" Artesia screamed out as he was losing his composure until the frat boy next to him downed his beer and squared up with Artesia. "Mellow out, dude." The frat boy kneed Artesia in the groin, and then went to another room mumbling to himself. "Stupid pledge."

Perneum walked inside and found the young man dressed as the devil working the trash can filled with red punch. "I don't think I got your name." Another frat boy dressed as an army soldier offered a friendly handshake. "It's dunk." Perneum was a little confused as a few people gathered around. "Dunk?"

"Yeah... DUNK!!" A group of guys grabbed Perneum and dunked him in the punch that was filled with a multitude of liquors and fruit punch. They pulled him back out. "Ya like that, butt pirate!?" Punch dripped from Perneum's face. "Not really..."

"Too bad, cause' we're gonna do it again!" They joyfully dunked him again, holding him under for a few seconds. Bubbles rose to the top as only his black boots protruded from the toxic punch.

Artesia tried to calm his frazzled nerves so he snuck a cigarette into the bathroom and promptly sat down on the toilet. The brief solitude and deep breath worked as he lit the cigarette and took a puff when there was a knock on the door. A nosy college girl could be heard outside. "Is somebody smoking in there?"
Artesia yelled back in a high-pitched voice, disguising his own.

"Of course not... Hold on!"

In a panic, he dropped the cigarette in the toilet and BOOM! He jumped around and tried to put the fire out on his butt. She leaned close to the door after hearing the ruckus inside. "You okay?"
He patted himself on the butt but it did little too extinguish the flames.

"Owww! Okay! Fine!" Artesia sat in the sink and frantically ran the water, much to his relief, until the sink collapsed under him and both he and the sink went tumbling to the ground. He rushed to straighten his costume and exit the bathroom, worried he might blow their cover. He quickly passed a party guy and girl as they waited patiently by the door and watched him scurry down the hall. They looked into the demolished bathroom as a plume of smoke rolled out.

"All you had to do was light a match, dude!"

Reid watched for Reece, who was dressed as Little Red Riding Hood, and stood in the back with her red hood down. She slowly looked up with those mysterious eyes that instantly captivated Reid. Without hesitation, he ran out and Benny grabbed at him, barely catching the back of his tan jacket. "Where are you going?"

Reid turned back and handed him his headphones. "If anybody asks for me, tell them I'm on break."

"You haven't even started." Benny whined.

Reid made his way swiftly through the crowd and to the back of the room to be with her. He took Reece's hand. "I'm so glad you made it." He started to take the hood off but she grabbed his hand.

"No."

"What's your name?" He asked.

"Reece." She whispered with a sparkle in her eye.

She was also consumed with his smile as she struggled to avoid his satisfied grin. She felt protected around Reid but was afraid for both of them.

"Want something to drink?" He offered but didn't want to leave her side. Reece looked around the room for Johnny. "I can't stay long because they always have someone following me."

Reid leaned close. "Who? Why?"

Johnny the Weasel dropped a round, yellow smiley mask over his face and tucked a gun into his belt as one of his goons followed him into the house.

The guys stood together as Perneum dripped with fruit alcohol punch and had a crooked smile on his face. Orco started working the room, looking high and low. He could sense that they were close. "We gotta find this guy." He walked up to Pervis, who was talking to a young lady, and pulled him away by his ear.

"We gotta talk about your etiquette. You see I was talking to the lady." Pervis complained as Perneum, drunk and staggering forward, fell flat on his face and briefly passed out. This was not going to be an easy task. Orco spotted Benny in the DJ booth. "I think we've found our man." Benny slapped a record on the turntable and Orco moved in front of the turntable. "It's time you come with us, Reid Wallace."

"Uh, I'm not Reid." Benny pointed at one of Alastor's goons, who was walking a few feet from Johnny the Weasel and in the middle of the room amongst partiers and a clump of girls dancing together.

"The guy you're looking for is right there." Benny pointed at the goon and shouted into the microphone. "How about a little disco!?" Benny ducked down but reached up and started the turntable.

Everybody jumped on the dance floor as Pierrot and Perneum made their way to the goon, following Orco's lead. Benny crawled off to warn Reid by working his way around the crowd. Artesia stood to the side of the dance floor keeping watch when Stella, the pale, goth girl in black from the sorority house, squeezed in beside him. "I'm not really into this crowd either." She looked closely at his forehead. "Your bead is sinking into your forehead. Yeah, this is sort of boring."

Stella pulled Artesia out on the dance floor and started to move with the music. Pervis gave a thumbs-up as Stella ran her hand over Artesia's chest and he was not sure what to do. She nudged him. "I saw you the other night."

Artesia did his best to ignore her. "No, you didn't." Uncomfortable, he tried to spot Orco, but Stella was persistent. "I knew a boy like you in the fourth grade."

"Orco!" Art cried out looking around the room for him and finally spotted the others. Stella looked down at his pants. "He constantly peed himself too."

Artesia tried to flag him down as he looked over the intoxicated crowd. Stella played with her gum, twisting it around her finger. "I dropped out in the fourth. Well, got kicked out for smoking, but" Artesia stuck his bony finger to Stella's mouth, quieting her. "I have to go. It was nice meeting you."

Orco made his way through the crowd as Johnny the Weasel walked from the opposite end. Johnny the Weasel pulled a gun out from behind his jacket. Perneum, acting fast, did a cart-wheel in front of Orco and Orco grabbed his feet. They moved one way, then the other together as Artesia and Pierrot moved in beside them. Stella moved seductively in front of them and Pervis led the crowd in clapping. "That's my boys!" They circled Stella, who danced in the middle and acted as though she cast a spell on Artesia, who fell back in Pierrot's arms. They were a hit with the crowd. The frat guys and sorority girls formed a circle around the dance floor and moved in beat to the song.

Johnny the Weasel screwed the silencer into the gun and his possessed finger immediately pulled the trigger. He looked around the room and then shrugged it off. Artesia felt his neck as blood ran down the side and Stella noticed and pointed. "You're like, uh, bleeding."

Artesia touched the wound again and wiped it on a frat boy's shirt who was dancing next to him. "It happens."

Reid leaned down to kiss Reece when Benny tapped him on the shoulder. He pointed at Orco. "They're looking for you."

Reece grabbed Reid's shoulder. "That's not them."

"Maybe they're disguised." Benny insisted.

"I'm telling you, that is not them." She persisted. Reid continued to gaze into Reece's eyes. He was only interested in being with her at the moment, regardless of the danger. "Play another song."

Johnny the Weasel crept onto the dance floor as the guys watched him closely and the crowd backed off. He signaled for one of his goons to go around the dance floor as another snuck up on Orco. Orco spun Perneum by the legs, who stretched out his arms, knocking out the goon and sending him sliding off of the dance floor. The crowd loved it and was pumped up to see more. Orco grabbed the goon and lifted him off of his feet as a frat boy led the crowd in a chant. "Fight! Fight! Fight!"

Johnny the Weasel stepped up to Orco while pointing his gun.

"We got no beef with you. We're just looking for the girl." Orco shoved the goon aside and squared up with Johnny the Weasel thinking he might be the one in charge.

A frat boy shoved Johnny the Weasel into Orco. "Gonna let him talk to you like that? Kick his butt!" Another frat boy pointed at Johnny and Orco gripped Weasel by the throat. The crowd chanted again. FIGHT! FIGHT! FIGHT!

Orco turned to the group, annoyed. "If you don't mind." and then back to Johnny the Weasel. Orco started his programmed speech. "Reid Wallace, I am here to read you your last rights-"

A girl pointed to the back patio. "What are you guys talking about? I just saw Reid out back." Orco, trembling mad with frustration and partly from the peer pressure, shoved Johnny the Weasel aside when another larger goon grabbed him. But Orco effortlessly, tossed him over the crowd. Johnny tucked his gun away and scampered off as Orco examined the wild crowd. "We've been double-crossed, boys! Where's Pervis!?"

Reid, standing in the back of the house and next to the patio, tried to kiss Reece, but she pulled away.

"I want to see you tomorrow," he told her, but she backed away even more, instinctively knowing they were being followed closely again. She feared there was nowhere to hide. "No more. It's too dangerous." Her eyes pled with him but Reid was not going to give up on her. "They can't be everywhere in Los Angeles."

"Oh, yes they can." Reece assured him and Orco was at the back door knocking patio furniture out of his way. He pointed in their general direction. Reid took her hand and they ran out of the back yard through a gate that led to the street. "I have a place."

Orco stepped forward and looked around with no luck.

"BURRRRPPP!" A drunk, short young man slapped Orco on the shoulder like they were long time friends. "Friends call me, Wildman." Orco shoved him aside by his face and looked out over the group of people who talked in the backyard. Perneum was right behind him and searched low. An irate Orco let out a hearty scream that sent a flame shooting off into the air and the partiers clapped for the show. A hired fire-blower approached them with his equipment in his arms and stomped his feet in frustration. "They did it to me again and sent someone else! I'm done with this job. Selling ice cream out of a truck wasn't so bad." He stormed off in a huff.

Pierrot and Artesia joined them as Stella walked out waving a small piece of paper. "I got his license plate if anyone cares."

AN UNLIKELY FRIENDSHIP

Sal sat at the table, took the bandaging off of his wing and examined the damage. Gus carried a lit candle to the table, throwing shadows in the old abandoned farmhouse. Sal worked the damaged wing in a circular motion and did his best to hide his pain. Could be worse, he thought.

"Looks like it's healing quite well. Probably be able to fly soon." Gus sat next to him on a bale of hay. "Speakin' of which, don't you have any special powers?"

Sal's wings drooped. "Oh, I can fly a little… But, not much anymore."

"How come?"

"Once we had a bad angel that flew the coop. Never came back. Up to no good, I assume, and abusing his powers. Since then they have sort of taken away most of our powers."

"Sorry to hear that." Gus consoled.

"I'm old, Gus… Not much left in the tank."

Sal's words resonated true with Gus who, judging by his somber expression, could deeply relate.

The light flickered off of Sal, casting a large silhouette against the barn wall with the wings reaching the bales of hay stacked above them. Gus taped the wing and looked over his work. "Sorry to hear that."

"Really doesn't matter. I'm on my last assignment anyway. Whole new young breed who travel by skateboard and parachute."

Gus offered a friendly handshake. "How bout' we make a deal? I'll help you if you help me. What do ya say, friend?"

Sal began to shake his hand but abruptly pulled away. "Friend? Remember the shooting incident. Hate to see how you treat your enemies!"

Gus jumped to his feet. "I let you use my truck."

"I stole your truck! And it's out of gas!"

Sal's free wing flared up and knocked the candle off of the table, igniting the other wing. Sal jumped around as Gus looked for something to extinguish the wing.

THE CHASE

Los Angeles, California

The zoo was bustling with families and couples racing from one animal exhibit to the next, enjoying the bright California day.

Reid handed Reece an ice cream cone as they felt like they could relax for the first time.

Artesia was the first one- "who would expect the zoo." They looked over the crowd as a scrawny security guard, whose khaki uniform was a couple of sizes too big, confronted Artesia for walking in without a ticket. Artesia growled, revealing bloody fangs that protruded from his devilish grin. The young, terrified security guard threw up his arms and dropped the gun which fired up at an angle. Artesia's head dropped and the security guard ran off and out of the park. Artesia felt the sharp pain in his shoulder and knew full well the bullet was once again meant for him. "Why? Why me?"

Stella called out with tickets in hand as she trotted forward. "I've got the tickets." She stopped and looked through the gaping hole in Artesia's shoulder to inspect the damage and saw Reid and Reece in the distance next to the monkey cage. "I think I spotted em'."

"Who would ever expect the zoo?" Reid took a lick off of his ice cream cone and Reece watched the monkeys that played with each other. They strolled to the gorilla exhibit to witness the newest addition, "The Beast". The huge gorilla beat his chest to make sure everyone knew he was the boss.

Reid took Reece's hand. Artesia snuck up behind them about to grab Reid, when he was pulled aside by "The Beast" who had reached through the bars. Reid and Reece happily moved along without noticing as Artesia was pulled into the cage. His bones crackled as a man pointed and laughed. "Ouch! That's gotta hurt!"

People crowded around as "The Beast" beat up on Artesia with his fists and jumped up and down on him, much to the crowd's delight.

Reid and Reece walked hand in hand by the rhino pit. The rhino looked her way and morphed into Alastor's face with gold horns. The rhino briskly spoke to her. "We'll find you, Reece."

She squeezed Reid's hand tight . "ARRGGHHH! Let's move on." Reece, wild-eyed, rushed away as Reid looked out into the rhino area confused.

"You okay?" He asked.

The guys snuck up on the opposite side of the fence and inside the exhibit as the rhino took off after them and Pervis ran away, though Orco grabbed him and tossed him safely to the opposite side. "This is not the way I should go!" Pervis dusted himself off and watched Perneum get bucked and tossed onto the roof of the rhino cage and Artesia taunted the rhino like a rodeo clown.

Reid looked back and focused on the Death Squad. "Those guys look familiar?" His eyes met with Orco's, who pointed at him until Orco was trampled.

The group scattered as the angry rhino chased Artesia and Reid and Reece made their way to the exit. They pulled out and onto the freeway, passing under a freeway sign listed, "Venice Beach take I-10 West".

Back at the mansion, Alastor screwed a gold horn into his head as the butler held a tray of horns in front of him. "Platinum is quite popular, sir." Alastor put it back and grabbed the platinum horn instead. He waved the butler off and turned to Johnny the Weasel.

"So, he's got protection?"

"What's a condom got to do with anything?" Johnny asked, confused.

"No, you shmuck! Strong arms!"

Johnny the Weasel began to light a cigarette but Alastor slapped it out of his hand. Johnny the Weasel continued. "Never seen these guys before."

"You sure they're working for him?"

Johnny the Weasel, animated, flailed his arms. "They picked up Manny the Meatball and trew him across the room."

Alastor rolled his eyes. "You mean '**threw**', Johnny, '**threw**'. What about Reece?" A dumbfounded expression spread across Johnny the Weasel's face.

"Oh yeah, her." Alastor, angry, jumped up. "I told you to keep an eye on her! She was at the zoo and heading toward Venice Beach!"

A stoic, Victorian painting of Reece sitting in a chair sat high above a fireplace behind them.

Traffic was stopped on crowded Sunset Boulevard in Hollywood. It slowly started to move again at a frustrating crawl as the Death Mobile inched down the busy street. A convertible Jaguar with an arrogant guy and his snobby girlfriend inside followed closely behind them. The arrogant dude honked his horn as he leaned out the side. "What's the holdup!?"

Smug, he turned to his girlfriend. "Wish they would take that thing to the East side where it belongs." He laid on the horn again for an extended length of time and then threw his hands up.

"Cmon!!"

A big ball of black goop was projected out of the exhaust pipe of the Death Mobile and covered the arrogant guy and his girlfriend, dripping down the side of the car. She grabbed at her hair and began to cry. "My hair!" And then him. "My hairpiece!"

Venice Beach, California

Reid and Reece skated on roller blades up to a female palm reader after rushing out of the zoo and decided to hang out at the popular tourist spot on the beach. "They promised they could help me get in the business. Offered me free room and board. He just seemed so harmless." She told Reid regarding the deceiving angel, Alastor.

"So, you moved out here to be a movie star? Let's find out if it's in your cards." Reid and Reece kneeled next to the woman who spread out her cards but also looked up to see who her new business was. "You're being followed."

Reid was shocked and impressed. "Dang, you're good. You haven't even looked at our cards yet."

The palm reader pointed. "No, I see you're being followed."

Reid grabbed Reece's hand as they skated off and Orco and the guys chased them. They turned down a crowded street lined with shops and restaurants until they saw an open door and disappeared into a building on the boardwalk. Orco waved at Pierrot and Artesia to go around the building.

Perneum pulled on the locked door of the building and then ran around the front. He walked into a weight room and looked around while holding up a small hatchet. An overly tanned, muscular man in shorts and tank top, stepped up to him. "Hey little buddy, we don't allow axes in here… Against the rules." The workout instructor pointed at a sign with a picture of an X over an axe. Perneum tossed it on the counter. He searched over the weight room and saw Reid and Reece duck into another room. He pulled out a long knife and the man waved at him with a big thumbs-up.

"More like it!"

Attractive and fit women kick boxed in the aerobics room that Reid and Reece ran through, weaving in and out, avoiding kicks and punches before reaching an exit door. Perneum, sneaking between bags, shoved a bag aside and was accidentally kicked in the groin, lifting him high off of his feet. He dropped to his knees and his head spun violently around. The apologetic woman looked down on him. "That looked like it really hurt, Mister."

Foam spilled out the side of his mouth, followed by violent convulsing.

"Are you gonna be okay?"

Perneum's eyes lit up beet red and loud grumbling could be heard from inside his heaving chest. She slapped icy hot between his legs and his eyes watered until he let out a blood-curdling scream and fell to his back staring up at the other women, who took pictures and video from their cell phones.

Next door in a small studio, a snobbish instructor stood in front of his acting class of eight bored students. He paced in front of the room.

"Would anyone like to perform Hamlet?"

Reid and Reece, out of breath, stood in the back looking for another exit when he pointed at them and sneered. "And we have two late ones who would like to volunteer."

Perneum jerked on the door and Reid took Reece's hand as they rushed to the stage. Reid immediately grabbed the script "Romeo and Juliet". He dropped down to his knees, and gazed into Reece's eyes. "Juliet, if I profance with my unworthy hand, this holy shrine, my lips ready stand."

She gently took his hand. "Good pilgrim, you do wrong your hand too much-"

Perneum stumbled down the aisle, exasperated and fuming with anger. Reece motioned to Reid with her eyes toward the back door and then continued reading from the script, "For Saints have hands that pilgrim's hands do touch, and palm to palm, is holy palmers kiss."

Perneum, fond of the theater from his days in England, brazenly made his way to the stage. Reid and Reece sat frozen in their spot as he took the opportunity to join in. He climbed up on the stage and went straight to the middle. "Why has thou forsaken me?" Perneum asked misty-eyed as he had also been known to re-write or add to his character as he saw fit. Reid and Reece looked at their scripts as the teacher slapped at his copy and looked for the line. "What is this?"

Perneum scowled at the teacher. "Hold thy tongue, scoundrel, or I will hold it for you." Perneum paced back and forth on the stage as the class watched and he had lost interest in Reid and Reece who were making their way to the edge of the stage and closer to the door. He clenched his fist and held it above him in dramatic fashion.

"Cowards die many times before their deaths."

The teacher, still looking over the script, stood over the short, violent angel. "Who are you?"

"The valiant never taste of death but once." Perneum grabbed the teacher by the throat, jerked him down to his level and then continued glaring into the teacher's eyes with a pained expression.

"Of all the wonders that I have yet heard, it seem to me most strange that men should fear."

Reid and Reece snuck out as Perneum went back stage, dragging the teacher with him. The class watched to see what would happen next as Reid and Reece safely made their way out of the building and back out on the boardwalk. Perneum walked back out with the professor's head in his hand.

A young man who was napping in the back, perked up. "Whoa... Awesome." He stood up and clapped and the others followed suit until a girl pointed. "Ugh, that's really his head." Screaming and panic ensued as Perneum tossed the head aside and looked around for Reid and Reece. He raced toward the door, shoving students out of the way and waving his shimmering knife.

Artesia walked down the middle of the Venice boardwalk when he was grabbed and jerked to the side. Stella was her usual self, decked out in black with heavy black eyeliner that stood out against her pale, white face. "I didn't know you like hanging out down here. I mean, I come down here some of the time but-" Artesia rolled his eyes and sat down as he knew this could take awhile.

Orco watched the frightened students run out of the building and looked up to see Reid and Reece sprinting toward a school bus parked next to the boardwalk. A teacher loaded up fourth grade Korean children who were all wearing matching blue school uniforms. The Korean children walked down the aisle of the school bus and Reid and Reece snuck in behind them. Orco peeked inside where the children were horse playing but with scissor kicks and karate chops to each other. He walked down the aisle, his boots thumped with every step as he studied their gazes.

"Alright!" He yelled to get their attention. (he moved his mouth but the words were delayed) "Have you... seen a man...and a woman..." The children laughed as he walked further down the aisle until he was hit in the back of the head with a small squid. Orco pulled his ears two feet out and his piercing eyes bulged out of their sockets. The students trembled and remained completely silent as a young Korean boy pointed to the back as Reid and Reece ran out the back door and Orco raced after them.

The crowd was thick at Venice Beach and Orco struggled to see around them as he stood next to the bus. "Oh, what the heck." Frustrated and thinking he might fly over the crowd, he spread his black wings and flapped while leaning forward but only fell on his face. Reece gasped as she and Reid were crouched under the bus. The bus pulled away and they were left squatting a few feet away from Orco. Orco reached out but a hot dog vendor wheeled in between them bumping over his big, bony knuckles and Reid and Reece were gone, ducking out once again.

A stray dog nipped at one of Artesia's exposed ribs. He swatted at the dog but it had already clung on to the exposed rib. "Beat it." Stella continued jabbering. "I don't like the kids at school; I mean they're not a lot of fun."

SNAP! The rib snapped off and Artesia lunged at the dog to get his rib back. "Hey!" The dog ran off with the bone in its mouth and quickly disappeared into the crowd with its prize.

Johnny the Weasel and a couple of his goons approached him.

"Where is she?" Johnny asked as his possessed finger went into Artesia's nose. Johnny pulled it out and forced the hand to his side. Stella, even for her standards, had a look of disgust. "You're gross."

"Where!?" Johnny demanded.

"I'd like to ask you the same question." Artesia asked him.

"Why would you ask me when I'm asking you?" Johnny the Weasel told him as they both thought about this for a brief moment and Artesia conceded. "Good point." Uncomfortable silence until-BAM! Johnny the Weasel went down and Pierrot held a large wooden mallet and was satisfied with her solid hit over his head. She proudly straightened her Viking horns and grinned. "Been awhile since I've done that."

Artesia jumped into a fighting stance and looked for something to grab. He broke off another rib and pointed it at them like a knife. The goons looked at each other after watching ooze from Artesia's side run down his leg and decided to safely run away as Johnny crawled on his knees trying to catch up with them.

The despondent dark angels walked down the sidewalk and bumped into the arrogant man, who was pulling out the last of the black glop in his hairpiece. The man abruptly turned. "Watch it, Jerk!" Orco stopped and walked back to the man. He cupped the man's head with his large palm waiting for the right vibe. The man swatted at Orco, who had the power of altering thoughts from the living. Something he learned from a Shaman while on assignment in Siberia.

"No touching the hair, jerkoff-" The man's eyes rolled back as Orco's mind powers had spread into the man's conscience and the man dropped to his knees. His body went completely limp. Orco wiped off his hands on the man's jacket and the man started to sob.

"Why me?"

His snobby and annoyed girlfriend nudged him hard and tried to get him to stand. She noticed the people watching her boyfriend blubbering and making a scene.

"Get up, you pathetic idiot."

He cried out to himself. "Why am I such a jerk!?" She grabbed his collar to lift him but he pulled away and continued. "And how did I get stuck with this miserable-?" She smacked him across the chin and spoke slowly through her teeth, emphasizing every syllable.

"Don't… you… dare… say it."

Orco saluted her with a broad smile and walked off.

DEFEATED

The Death Mobile cruised down the street with the group inside and in an evil mood, frustrated at losing Reid. Perneum had his feet propped up and he kept clicking the automatic door lock until Artesia slapped his hand from the back. "Stop it or die, Troll." Pierrot looked over at Artesia. "That's not near as bad as you picking at your ribs all day. Pick, pick, pick!" Pierrot reached over, as if to pick at Artesia and accidentally hit Pervis in the nose, who in turn smacked Perneum in the back of the head. "You started all this!" Perneum reached over and put Pervis in a headlock as Artesia and Pierrot fought in the back. Perneum's eyes glowed red and his face became demonic. Pierrot's tongue lashed out at Artesia as he exposed his skull.

A family wearing mouse ears and deer horn hats sat in their car terrified at the stoplight as they watched the quarreling of dark angels. They watched as small flames shot in every direction that were accompanied by long tongues that smashed against the windshield. The father floored it and weaved in an out of traffic. "Last time we come to Los Angeles... Last time!!"

Inside the Death Mobile, eyeballs were flung back and forth and fire scorched the roof. Orco looked back and slapped the seat. "I'll stop this car right now!!" The guys straightened up after a couple of more slaps. Orco looked forward again and gripped the steering wheel, the white of his knuckles showed as he did his best to conceal his growing anger as he headed to the cemetery. "Just wait till' we get home!" He was all out of answers and grew tired of their incompetence, if not his own.

A long, clear tube ran out of a cemetery plot in the ground. Scientists in lab coats put a little solution in the tube. The scientist tapped the tube lightly. "Use sparingly," another scientist reminded him.

The green solution traveled slowly down the tube and into a coffin with a newly deceased man lying inside. Headlights flashed in the distance from the approaching Death Mobile and the scientists quickly gathered up their stuff. “Let’s get out of here.”

The scientists tossed their bags in a van and raced off down a dirt road.

The Death Mobile passed the van and then screeeech! It came to a halt and Orco exited in a huff, slamming the door shut behind him. The gargoyle hood ornament covered its eyes. Orco, red-faced, turned to the Death Mobile hood ornament. “And I don’t want anything out of you! …**NOTHING**!!” Artesia stepped out and moved around to Perneum, glaring down at him. “Did you sabotage this one too!?”

“I told you I was done with that.” Perneum fired back.

Artesia’s wasn’t completely convinced. “Where were you?”

“Where were you, genital wart?” asked Perneum.

Now Orco turned to both of them. “What did I tell you!?” Artesia turned his anger at Orco. “You know you have led us down a path of destruction and you let the snitch foul everything up.”

Perneum and Artesia started to wrestle as Perneum lunged forward and grabbed his leg. Orco did his best to break them up as Pierrot ran around the car, grabbing Artesia around the throat and tried to pull him off. The Death Mobile started to bounce up and down and then rolled over the guys with Stella and Pervis inside.

Stella leaned out of the window. “That looked like it hurt… Sorta.” Orco stretched out his sore back, letting out a weak moan.

“Serves us right. We can’t handle this one.”

There was no argument from the group, who got back to their feet and the hunchback crawled into a grave beneath the Death Mobile. Orco went back to looking over the list as Pervis paced anxiously in front of them.

“Why are you guys keeping me around?”

“You’re not having fun?” Artesia sarcastically joked as he whittled a small limb into a rib and tried it on for size, though it was still too long. The hunchback, changing the oil underneath the Death Mobile, handed a credit card swiper to Orco, who knelt beside the car. “Might want to use lighter-weight oil next time,” Orco signed the credit card slip and handed it back as the zombie tried to climb out of the grave behind them but slid back in, sending dirt and rocks piling on top of him.

"Why weren't you at your post!?" Orco asked Perneum.

"You think I missed him?" Perneum protested as the others listened for an answer and Pervis became inpatient, fearing the worst. "Why are you guys holding me?!"

"You're of no help anyway!" Perneum stood on a tombstone and held an axe above Pervis' head but Orco stepped in front of him.

"Back off Per."

Perneum fumed with anger. "Why Per and not Perneum? You think that because I'm a third of your size that you can call me Per?"

The zombie tried again and his rigid fingers buried themselves like a hoe in the soft ground as he tried to hoist himself up. The guys were oblivious to him and still awaited an explanation from Perneum. Now, even Orco had turned on Perneum. "We've had a perpetual stroke of bad luck with you!"

Exasperated, Pervis demanded, "For the last damn time... Why are you guys holding me?!!!"

"Because you're on the list for February!" Perneum blurted out but regretted it because they needed his help and had decided to keep this bad news from him until they finished their assignment. Pervis, devastated, staggered a little in disbelief, weaving between tombstones and staring at the ground. Pierrot showed a mother's touch and put her hand on his shoulder but he lightly brushed it away and plopped down next to a tombstone.

Pervis ran his hand along the deceased name and wondered about the grieving family he left behind. He thought about their expectations from when this person was a child but it only reminded him of his own failures.

Perneum tried to show a softer side to the group. He spoke in a soft tone as his arms hung limply at his side. "You're right. I was Lucifer's right hand man, but I've never sabotaged a mission. I've even tried to leave a few times so I wouldn't be responsible for anything that went wrong. Didn't want to let you guys down."

The zombie could barely pull himself out as the others failed to notice. They were still trying to figure out who was at fault, despite it being just bad luck compounded by ineptitude. The zombie was halfway out as Pervis, who was back on his feet, made his way back toward the group and accidentally stepped on the zombie's hand. The zombie checked the hand for broken bones and tried to pull himself up further with very little luck.

Pervis sat on the hood of the Death Mobile and stroked the gargoyle's head collecting a mild purr. "What will I tell my mother?"

Orco scratched his head. "I'm gonna try to get us a new assignment." Perneum held his luggage and a chainsaw, ready to leave the group. "It's too late. If this is what you guys think of me, then I'm sorry for all the troubles I've caused. Now you won't ever have to deal with me again."

Orco felt bad for the little guy but thought that maybe it would be better if he went out on his own.

The zombie rubbed his arm like he needed a fix as Perneum unknowingly kicked him, which sent him tumbling back down into the grave. Perneum, hoping someone would talk him out of leaving, looked up at the moon and then moved to a small area where the moon's reflection met an engraving on a rusted copper sundial that rested on top of a large marble slab.

Orco struggled with the idea of losing Perneum and finally relented."Per, wait!" Perneum looked up in time to reach out for Orco but the moon's glow hit squarely on the dial and the ground dropped below him, sending Perneum plummeting through the earth at a rapid pace. The earth burped, sending rocks and dirt flying up and then it was closed.

Artesia sulked by a tombstone when Stella walked over to console him.

"I knew the munchkin would run,"

She winked as she nuzzled up next to him. "Open your mouth and stick out your tongue." He slowly revealed a forked tongue and Stella was evidently quite impressed. "Cool." They kissed.

Orco clapped his hands together. "Hey, you know what will cheer us up?"

PIZZA, EYEBALL AND DAMNATION

The waitress in the small family owned pizzeria in Los Angeles, waited patiently for Orco to place his order as she tapped her pen against the pad. He shoved the menu aside. "Pepperoni with extra fire sauce." She scribbled the order down and trotted off as Orco became glum and thought out loud. "Extra fire sauce was Perneum's favorite. Extra fire sauce." Orco pounded his clenched fist on the table. The thought of Perneum leaving evidently was too much. "Durn him."

Pierrot slammed her empty beer mug down and signaled for another as the guys sat sullenly staring down at the table and Artesia grabbed at his face. "I'm blind!"

The people sitting around them moved toward the door and Orco pointed at Artesia's eyes. "You have them on backwards." Artesia popped his eyeballs back out, put one back in the eye socket and fumbled with the other until it squirted out of his hands. It rolled across the tile floor and was almost squashed by a waitress who stepped over it as she delivered a pizza to the next table.

Artesia frantically crawled across the floor bumping head first into chairs and almost had it when he reached out for the eyeball but a frightened woman screamed and kicked it across the room. He scrambled to make it to the other side as it flew onto the pizza pan on the line ready to go out. The busy waitress grabbed the pan and walked it out to the Death Squad's table.

Orco plopped his crossed arms on the table. "I led a life of crime but I never stole from old ladies." He looked Pervis' way.

"It's not like I took anything of value," remarked Pervis.

"A stereo has value." Artesia told him, squinting and fumbling his way back to the table.

"And what does an old lady need with a stereo?" Pervis asked them as he surveyed all of their disappointed expressions. He wasn't going to win this one and he knew it.

The waitress set the pizza on the table complete with eyeball. Artesia took the eyeball out, licked it, and put it gingerly back in its socket. He looked around as one eye pointed the opposite direction of the other but was satisfied to get his eye back. Orco waved at the waitress. "More hot sauce." She pulled one off of a table, delivered it, and took a step away without taking her eyes off of them. Orco took a lit match to his slice of pizza as they watched the flames almost reach the roof.

Stella dabbed her finger in the ice water and then turned to Art.

"You have a little tomato sauce on your eye, honey," and then to Orco, "What about you, Orca?"

"That's Orco, thank you. Ran the guillotine at the gallows."

Pervis laughed to himself. "And I bet you did a good job at it."

"Actually, I was quite a failure. Had a meltdown. Slapped the King and his jester down and, well the blade fell and the king walked with a limp and the jester…" He pondered this for a moment. "I guess I did okay with him because he was beheaded."

"Great story." Pervis sullenly told them as his stomach turned but he grabbed a slice of pizza anyway and turned it sideways, checking it for any body parts. Pierrot slapped Pervis on the shoulder. "You might be working with us… Permanently."

Orco was quick to intervene. "Now don't say that. We are going to retire and Pervis might miss his expiration date."

Stella, not done with Orco, waved her finger at his jacket wanting an explanation. "What's with the all-male biker bar attire you see at rainbow rallies?"

"I was given a second chance and hung with Kerouac in the fifties." He straightened his collar and ran his fingers through his greasy hair.

"Sent a motorcycle off a cliff in Malibu with me on it." Pervis pointed at Artesia, who was still trying to sort out his eye. "What about him?"

They all squirmed a little. Pierrot grabbed a cheese stick. "He's a birth defect of nature."

"Just a cold blooded killer, huh?" Pervis suggested.

"No, a birth defect… Look at him."

Pervis studied Artesia and agreed with a nod of the head. Artesia looked up with cheese dangling from his chin. He grunted and continued to eat.

Pierrot was eager to give her story. "Me, a Viking and a petty thief. Torched a few vessels... (her eyes lit up) And a few ex-boyfriends." She giggled to herself but Pervis was still interested in their story.

"And the little guy's a snitch."

Orco put his slice down. "Yeah, thought I could help correct his ways. Oh, well, huh? Can't save em' all." Orco took a drink through the multi-colored straw as he pondered the good times with Perneum.

"So, what happens if we don't find this guy?" Pervis asked and Orco took a deep breath and then looked him squarely in the eyes.

"We are doomed to hell."

"What if we succeed?"

"The alternative is that we earn our wings. Visited by Iris." Orco gladly told him.

"Wings? Iris?" Pervis asked.

Pierrot glowed. "Heaven. Where we are all beautiful creatures... Well, potentially."

"And if you save enough lives, you move into the kingdom," Orco cheerfully added, briefly pondering what eternal bliss would be like. Pervis put peppers on his pizza and was a little more at ease. "Not a bad trade-off."

"Either that or we are condemned to hell, fire and brimstone for an eternity." The sobering thought caused Orco's shoulders to slump as he finished. "Together."

Pervis' ears perked up and the hair on the back of his neck stood on end. "We need a plan."

NO TURNING BACK

Mojave Desert, California

The dry, hot wind blew against a tree off of the interstate in California. Sal peddled the bicycle with Gus on the handle bars. "This ain't gonna work." Sal struggled to keep the wobbly bike moving straight as Gus did his best to stay still. "Try to keep her steady."

They looked out over the endless highway in front of them until Sal stopped. "Why is it so damn important that you ruin my prophecy?" Gus became somber as he hopped off of the bike. "I want to go back with you. All the way." Sal pointed up as he walked with the bike. "You mean?" Gus looked down and couldn't find the words at the moment. "Why would you want that?" Sal asked.

Gus kicked at the dirt. "Got my reasons."

They started walking side by side next to the bicycle and Sal began to understand. "Someone you miss, huh?"

PERNEUM FINDS HIS WAY

Hell

Lucifer, Prince of darkness and evil on earth and below, walked away as Perneum followed closely behind him. "Always complaining. Never happy. Never ever."

Perneum struggled to keep up with him. "You gave them an unfair assignment." Lucifer stepped on a head buried in the ground; firmly planting his heal on the scalp. "Why do you care?"

Perneum didn't need to put much thought into it. "They're my friends."

Lucifer continued, "I can use you here. Natural disasters, diseases, searching for new reality show contestants…"

Perneum made his way in front of Lucifer. "They need me."

"You're being serious? You of all demons. Don't do this to me. I don't deal well with guilt."

Lucifer led Perneum away by the shoulder then acted as if he wanted to take Perneum's photo. "Take a step back so I can capture this moment." Perneum shuffled back, forcing a grin as Lucifer signaled a little further. Perneum inched back even further and was just about at the right spot when Lucifer signaled a tiny bit more. Perneum stepped back and fell through the earth.

Lucifer looked down the hole. "When you get to the bottom, go due east and follow the weeping trees. Weeping trees!!"

Even his conscience occasionally got to him. "I don't get paid for helping!" He pulled the hair of a protruding head out of the ground and plucked at the hair like a harp. "What was Gabe thinking?" He plucked harder. "Now it's my problem!?"

He held up a cheese grater and looked down at the head. "Like me to massage your scalp?"

LOST THEIR FAITH IN ORCO

The Death Mobile pulled up to the cold cemetery, down a dirt road to their usual spot on an overcast night. The hunchback filled a shallow grave with dirt and Orco handed him some money for rent as he pulled through. The groundskeeper licked his over-inflated lips with a freakishly wide tongue as he counted the money.

"Gotta go see the big man." Orco mentioned and the gravedigger slapped the money into his Velcro wallet. "Try not to stay away too long."

The mood was somber as they exited the car with waning hope. They knew better than to trust Orco and get their hopes up again.

Artesia, prepared for the worst, took Stella by the hand and decided to go for a short walk. She gladly accepted as they walked down a trail that led past a mausoleum. He stopped and decided to deliver the bad news. "I have to say goodbye."

Heartbroken and confused, Stella put her hand to his bony cheek. "What do you mean, Arty?" A tear welled up in her eye and started to make its way down her cheek but he was there to catch it with his finger. He flashed her a comforting smile. "You don't want to be around us when we get back. It's better that way." She held on tight to the only man, or at least dark angel, she'd ever loved who loved her back.

Orco, Pierrot, and Artesia stood in a circle holding hands around the sun dial and waited for the moon to cast its glow in the middle and over the metal eye. The clouds were thick as the moon fought to shine through, but had little luck. Orco pulled away thinking it was a bad omen and was ready to give up when the cloud dispersed and the moonlight, much brighter than usual and almost blinding, aimed at its target and the earth began to shake beneath them and gave away below.

"Hold on, boys!...Girls!" Orco screamed out as they dropped through the earth, painfully bouncing off layer after layer of earth at a rapid speed.

Bristol, England

Meanwhile, in a school in England, a tall male teacher with a button-down shirt under a navy blue sweater vest, pointed at a model of the earth and its layers. "As you can see nothing could survive the intense heat, miles under the earth's surface." He tapped the model a couple of times.

"The heat alone would burn you to bloody ashes."

The fifth grade children, stunned, watched the Death Squad falling with their hair on fire down the model of the earth. One student pointed at the model. The teacher continued as he glanced over his shoulder. "Except, I suppose the evil dead themselves." The children were speechless except one who put on his glasses and muttered, "Blimey, Sir."

The guys fell on the ground bruised, beaten and still on fire as Lucifer, who acted as if he were expecting them, stood close by with a couple of wooden mallets in his hands. A deformed creature dragged itself over with a bucket of water that constantly spilled over the edge. Orco, gagging for water, picked it up and looked inside but there was only a drop left. He poured it over his head as the others did their best to put out the flames on their heads. Orco handed the bucket back. "Uh, thanks."

"You guys just missed Perneum," Lucifer mentioned disconcertedly.

"Seems he's done with this mission and back with you." Orco told him, hoping he was wrong.

The guys sat in three chairs facing Lu, who pointed at the ground.

"Guys want to see what I've been working on?!"

He went to the live human heads that were resting above the ground just above the neck. He tapped on one head with the mallet. A demon pulled the hair straight up from another head and played it like a bass.

"Need a little more practice but here it goes." Lucifer played on the head, trying to find his rhythm. BONK, BONK, BONK, CLINK, CLINK, he whacked the head's ear and the head winced in pain. "OWWWWWW!" BONK! BONK!

Lucifer danced around the head and hit it one more time but it sounded hollow. The head looked up with its mouth wide open and

Lucifer glared down on it. "What happened to your brains?"

"I dunno?"

"Guess who just became my bowling ball?" Lucifer happily told him.

"Oh, boy."

Lucifer seemed to be enjoying this as the group waited impatiently and did their best to act interested. Orco sprung up and stepped forward. "Sir, if I could-"

Lucifer stepped on another head. "Shad up!" The other heads looked up at Orco as if pleading not to speak out again and Orco took a step backward, falling back in the chair. Lucifer started in again. "This was your *big* chance for redemption and you guys seem to have blown it." Orco looked at his group. They were tired and mentally beaten down.

"Twenty four hours. If we fail then, I'll join the living dead," Orco said, studying over his group. "I failed em', so let them go." Artesia started to speak but Pierrot, okay with Orco's agreement, grabbed Art's tongue and accidentally pulled it out. She apologetically handed it back. Lucifer rolled his eyes. "Where is your assignment!?"

Orco pulled out the wadded-up scroll and handed it to him. Lu looked it up and down.

"There's bird crap on this!" Artesia subtly tried to get his attention but had difficulty speaking without a tongue. "We dink dit's a 'I'."

"Have you talked to Gabriel?" Lucifer asked them.

They looked at each other with no answer in mind, which frustrated Lucifer even more and the heads tried to sink further down past their ears.

"Of course not, that's why you have been sent to me." He looked over the scroll and the walls shook until Lucifer started to chuckle, then built into full-blown deranged laughter. Orco and the group joined in as well and the heads also rang out with laughter. Lucifer stopped abruptly. "You morons have got the wrong person."

Artesia stuck his tongue back in his mouth and adjusted it.

"We're thoomed."

Lucifer waved his finger at Artesia. "Watch how you use that word around here… Serious." He handed the scroll back to Orco.

"You guys don't stand a chance in hell... Or earth!" He found this funny again as his evil, roaring laughter was followed by coughing, which was then followed by a lengthy, slimy throat clearing that disgusted the group.

A twelve-foot hour glass was lifted by demons and then THUMP!, set back down on a few heads.

Lucifer sat down on a collection of heads. "Twenty four hours and you're mine… Not that I really want ya. Hell, I'm even pullin' for ya."

Lucifer winked and made a lewd tongue gesture as the guys moved to their positions and tried to avoid his glares and hungry look. A head looked up at the guys. "It's hell on the back."

Lucifer pulled a lever and they were ejected back up, crashing back through the earth.

Highway 40, California

Gus hitchhiked as Sal hid in the bushes for what seemed like a small eternity.

The sweltering heat beat down on them as two elderly ladies, barely able to see over the dashboard, pulled up in an old, rusted gray car. "Just need a lift up the road a piece," Gus told them as the feeble old ladies looked at each other and then back at Gus. "We don't have much gas and very little money."

Gus pulled out his wallet with understanding eyes. "I could help a little with gas."

The little old lady with the flowery hat swiped the wallet from his hand and they sped down the highway. Gus chased after the car for only a brief moment before giving up, winded from the quick but short sprint.

The now-empty wallet was thrown back out the window and Sal trotted over to retrieve it, joining Gus. "Sort of makes you wonder why I do my job."

Gus was still doubled over out of breath.

"There are a few good people out there."

Sal handed Gus his wallet and looked around at the vast nothing along the highway. "Where?!"

Gus looked inside the empty and bare wallet containing only a picture of a pretty woman with dark, curly hair. Saddened, he tucked it back into his back pocket. "We need to concentrate on making bus fare."

He pulled out some change and Sal noticed as his wings drooped.

"We're broke."

REECE'S SECRET

Close to midnight in the mansion, Reece carried her shoes as she tiptoed softly down the hall in her socks when she heard voices in the boardroom.

She stopped to listen as Alastor sat in the next room with a scientist and talked about her doomed fate and the need for her blood to give the zombies a thirst for more blood. Her face went white as she quickly scurried away, past a snoozing guard. She dodged down another hallway, accidentally stepping on the hand that reached out from under the stairwell. She looked in all directions before rushing out of the front door, unnoticed.

The mansion grounds were still heavily guarded as Reece crawled behind the bushes on the front porch and toward the corner of the yard where Reid awaited on top of the wall for her.

She was trapped as a guard stood between her and Reid. She tossed a pebble at a window and the guard turned, almost firing his but put the firearm down and decided to investigate. She scurried along the side of the mansion and across the yard. She reached the wall as a shot was fired her way, zinging off of the concrete wall as Reid helped her up and over.

They raced to Benny and the awaiting car, quickly hopping inside. Benny floored it and the car raced down the street, swerving out of control, narrowly missed a fire hydrant. The car stopped and Benny and Reid calmly exchanged places and then proceeded forward.

The sign promoting "rooms by the hour" flickered on and off at the sleazy, run-down motel off of Ventura Blvd in North Hollywood. Reece, Reid, and Benny sat at a table with only a candle lighting the room as they attempted to stay low-key and hidden from Alastor's goons. Reid spoke directly to Reece. "So, they want the rest of your blood?"

Benny looked like he was going to be sick to his stomach.

"I heard them say that they plan on sacrificing me tomorrow at midnight."

Benny grabbed her arm. "We have to get her out of here!" Reid shoved him away. "How about those crazy guys that are trying to kill me?"

"I swear I don't know them."

"What makes you the chosen one?" Reid asked.

Benny looked up at Reece and she looked over at Reid, embarrassed. "I'm a virgin."

Reid immediately grabbed Benny's jacket and assisted him up. "See ya, Benny." Reid took her hand. "I'm taking you far from here."

They were quick to gather their stuff and leave when Benny opened the door and let out a shrill scream. Johnny the Weasel stood at the threshold of the door next to a zombie who still had lines on his face from laying sideways in the coffin and a brown afro wig that hung to the side. It was only when the newly-dead zombie caught his reflection in the mirror that it bothered him and he turned the wig from side to side as Johnny the Weasel pointed at Reece. "You're coming with us!"

Johnny's possessed hand went down behind the zombie and the zombie's eyes lit up and his afro stood on end. Frustrated with the out-of-control hand, he took a deep breath and pulled his possessed hand away. Boink! Johnny the Weasel forced a step back and fumed with anger. "NOW!!"

Reid stepped forward and two zombies stomped inside. He quickly grabbed for anything he could find and swung a lamp, knocking one back, but it regained its balance and slowly crept forward. Reid screamed at Reece to go out the back and through the bathroom as two more zombies walked inside. Reece plead with Johnny the Weasel. "I don't want to see anyone get hurt."

"Too late for that," warned Johnny.

Benny fended off another zombie, whose tongue licked his scalp, hungry for brains.

"Can I get some help here?" Benny cried out as he was shoved aside by Johnny the Weasel.

Johnny grabbed the zombie and tossed him outside the room by the collar. Reece stepped up to the side of the bathtub as a zombie crawled through the bathroom window and she ran back out into Johnny the Weasel's awaiting arms. Reid lunged forward but was grabbed from behind by a zombie as another one descended on him and opened his mouth wide to bite the flesh out of Reid's arm.

Johnny pulled out his gun, aimed and shot twice. The zombies rolled off; feeling the large, gaping holes in their heads as Johnny pulled Reece away.

Johnny the Weasel slammed the door shut behind him, but the finger decided to stay inside. "Ooooooowwwww!" He opened the door and rushed to catch up with the zombies.

Reid and Benny ran to the window and helplessly watched Johnny toss Reece into the car.

Gus and Sal stood arm in arm in front of a tavern off of the main interstate and sang a Broadway tune together. A couple walking into the bar dropped some change in a cup at Sal's feet. The unwitting performers scrambled to see how much money they had earned.

A few minutes passed as Sal and Gus stood a few feet from each other and a small crowd had gathered. Gus, overacting, threw his arms up and looked at Sal as they did their best Abbott and Costello routine. "Who's on first?" They threw their arms around each other and then they belted out at the same time: "Third base!" A little more change was dropped in the cup as the people dispersed.

They huddled around the money. Sal pulled out the dollar bills while Gus counted the loose change. "How much we got?" Gus asked as a disappointed grubby man stood to the side scratching his large belly. "I thought I requested Cher."

The long night had drawn to an end as Sal counted the change in the can and Gus, wearing makeup and a dress, glanced over at the limited amount.

"How much we got now?" Gus asked.

"Not enough for bus fare."

Gus pulled out a gold locket from his pocket. "Probably get something for this." Sal leaned close and looked over the locket and the faded picture of a pretty woman with curly, dark hair.

"She's the one, huh?"

"Yep." Gus hung his head and Sal put his arm around him.

"You sure you want to do this?" Sal asked as Gus took a deep breath and perked up a little, forcing a small smile. "All the way, Sal."

The bus pulled up and Gus gripped the locket tight. Sal let him lead the way as he went up the steps of the bus. "I appreciate your help," Gus told him.

"Let's go get our guy," Sal added as the door closed behind them.

THE ANCIENT BURIAL GROUND

Perneum walked through a long, dark tunnel that finally opened to a misty, open field surrounded by Japanese weeping cherry trees. The trees created a wall around a burial ground with horses in war dress and Samurai warriors frozen in their chosen spot.
He stepped out into the large burial ground observing the once colorful Japanese war costumes on top of decorated armored horses, but now had faded with the passing hands of time.

"Where am I?" Perneum asked himself while running his hand along the lining in the horses' dressing.

"You almost fall to China," said a voice behind him. Perneum abruptly turned, swinging his knife and narrowly avoiding a little, old Asian wise man perched on a tombstone.

"What is this place?" Perneum asked.

"You already ask that." The man nibbled on a small block of cheese.

"Who are these people or things?" Perneum stood beside a horse and the wise man straightened the armor. "The dead... Souls suspended in armor. Great warriors at one time."
"Sorry to hear that," said Perneum, "How do I get back up top?"

Perneum grabbed a sword but the stoic Samurai jerked it back. The wise man studied Perneum up and down. "You ask a lot of questions."

"Listen, old man. I'm on a tight schedule."

"Long road back." The wise man told him while taking a small portion of cheese and slipping it into his mouth.

Perneum squared up with the man. "I have for the first time in my life... err, and death, found people who are relying on me to do the right thing."

"Touching. Put it in a Christmas card." The wise man gave a muffled laugh.

"Charming piece of work you are," said Perneum, who was now looking for a way out.

"These soldiers and their horses also fought for glory, but their services are needed no more. Maybe, you end up like them."

"I've, uh, known you for less than two minutes and I really don't like you." Perneum watched him pick at his toenails with no regard for anything else at the moment.

THE EXPERIMENT

Alastor paced in front of a cage of zombies who played cards with each other. He was followed by the scientists, action hero, Rock Gentry, and various world leaders. An exterminator with coke bottle glasses walked down the hall with the squirrel clinging to his back.

"Is there still a problem or do you think you can fix it?" Alastor asked him and then opened the cage.

The exterminator was all business as he rattled off- "Blood–thirsty zombies waiting on their virgin blood and chemical fix just so that they can destroy the human race and replace them with mindless, obedient masses of deteriorating flesh and bone?" He had a look of grave concern and then continued, "I say you got a problem, sir. Glad ya called me when you did."

He pulled out an order pad and Alastor pointed at the cage.

"Could you just check out this little problem?"

The exterminator, squinting through his thick glasses, looked closer and was shoved in the cage and the zombies attacked him.

"This is gonna cost extra!"

The cage, shaking and rattling, was locked behind him and Johnny the Weasel walked in with Reece. Alastor jubilantly went to them. "It won't be long now, my darling. Just one more vial of blood."

There was an uncomfortable silence for a moment as Johnny the Weasel looked over at Reece and then at Alastor. "You were, uh, referring to her as darling weren't you?"

The preparations were made and the time had finally come and Alastor was ready. Johnny the Weasel wore a metal glove to contain the possessed hand and held Reece with the other hand. The scientist held a vial up and squirted a couple of drops out. "We just need the test subject."

Evil men gathered around a dead man on a table as a couple of zombies took Reece and pulled her to the side.

Alastor licked his lips with his forked tongue as he anxiously waited. His dream and obsession would soon become a reality.

"The blood of an innocent virgin," he told them and Johnny the Weasel dropped to his knees laughing at the "virgin" comment but Alastor was not amused. "Get up, you idiot!"

Johnny the Weasel tried to dry his tears as he got to his feet but was still a little hunched over from the uncontrollable laughter. "I love these guys."

Johnny punched himself in the nose with the possessed finger in the metal glove and dropped against the floor again. He ripped off the glove and tossed it aside as he writhed in pain.

The needle was stuck into Reece's arm and blood drained rapidly into it. The beaker was mixed with another solution and a drop of blood was added. The mixture smoked and a small yellow greenish ghost hovered above it. Alastor swatted at it and then turned to the scientist. "A little heavy on the citric acid."

The small ghost barked at Alastor, snapping at his face. Alastor simply waved his hand and the ghost was gone. "Apply it!"

Johnny the Weasel, still laughing, got to his knees again and then grabbed the syringe with his "out of control hand." He jabbed himself with it, then dropped flat on his back. Alastor grabbed at the syringe. "Give me that, you moron!" Alastor jerked it out of his arm and Johnny the Weasel reached up and grabbed Alastor's groin with the possessed hand.

Johnny the Weasel's face lit up. "Cough twice."

Alastor squealed in pain and then broke away. He handed the syringe to the scientist, "Burn this one!" Alastor spoke to nobody in particular, "Give him another needle."

The scientist stuck the needle in the dead guy's arm and applied the toxin. Everyone curiously gathered around as neon green lit up the veins that pulsated inside the convulsing body. The dead guy sprung up with his upper body. "Howdy! Gonna be clear as a bell with a little hint of rain in the forecast for later on this week."

Alastor leaned close to the scientist. "Whose blood did you draw?"

"I was rushed. I, uh-- Johnny the Weasel gave it to me!" The scientist complained as Alastor slammed his fists on the table. Johnny the Weasel was oblivious to everything around him at the moment and swatted at imaginary flies.

"What is with you guys?" Alastor complained as the

exterminator moved close to the bars. "Ask him if it's gonna rain or not. Gotta big job in Phoenix."

"Shut up!" Alastor regained his composure. "This is only a test, folks." Alastor, frustrated, paused and then continued. "We'll eventually have zombies who will have the thirst for blood and will be able to think for themselves- Hey!"

A zombie squatted in the corner of the room. Alastor pointed down the hall. "Bathroom is first door on the left!"

He turned to Reece who was still struggling with the mindless zombies.

"Now where are your friends? The ones like me?" Alastor asked. She continued to try to free herself from their grip.

"I don't know who you're talking about."

TIME TO WORK TOGETHER

Pierrot brushed and checked her decayed teeth in the rear view of the Death Mobile as Orco threw his clothes in a suitcase. "What are you do doing?" She asked.

Artesia and Stella crawled out of the back seat also noticing Orco's erratic behavior. Orco grabbed his weapons. "Go with me to Haight Ashbury. Maybe even Montana. Heck, I've never been to Cancun." Orco rushed around the cemetery grabbing what he could find. Artesia pulled Orco's chainsaw away from him. "We're not done here, Orco!"

"Tired of fighting it! I've had enough." Orco let him have the chainsaw and he grabbed for an axe.

He studied the blade and then tossed it in the suitcase. "Don't leave us now, Orco." Pierrot begged of him.

Artesia pulled on Orco's jacket. "I want to earn my wings!"

Orco slammed his luggage shut with clothes and snakes hanging out of the sides. "THAT IS TOTALLY OUT OF THE--!"

"I need your help." Reid walked up and the guys stood frozen in their tracks. Orco turned. "Can it be?" Pierrot and Artesia reached for their weapons with evil in their eyes but Reid continued forward.

"I know what you guys are thinking."

Stella tried to warn him with the "throat slash" gesture and shoosh him away. "Oh, no you don't," she told him as she pretended to be choking, then shooting herself in the head, and then hanging as the group noticed and she finally stopped.

Pierrot held a large sledgehammer and Reid stood a few feet in front of them. "My girlfriend is in grave danger."

"Don't think I would worry about your girlfriend, right now." Stella told him as she put a large plastic sheet over her head.

The guys surrounded him and the gargoyle hood ornament trembled with fear. Orco pointed a bazooka at Reid as Pierrot held her sledgehammer high above Reid's head and Artesia foamed at the mouth with a huge grin. Orco glanced over at Artesia. "You gonna get ready, or what?"

Artesia cleaned his mouth off with his sleeve. "Oh, yeah…

Sorry." He picked up the chainsaw, fired it up and waved it in the air. Reid dropped to his knees. "You have the wrong guy! Please!"

Sal and Gus ran up, waving their arms. "Stop!"

A crow landed beside them on a tombstone. Sal spoke gently to the crow. "Your job is done. Where is your brother?"

Sal glanced at the ground where only a pair of crow's legs from earlier lay. He assisted Reid up and then reached down to pick up a note on the ground that read, *"You have the wrong person... stupid."* He fumed with anger as he looked toward Orco. "**You**!!"

Orco seethed red with anger as he stomped toward Sal.

"Ever since I ran into you my luck has been sour!"

Sal flapped his wings and rushed straight toward Orco, who flapped his large black wings, eager to meet half-way.

"You moron!" Sal screamed out as they grabbed each other by the throat. Sal tightened his grip on Orco's throat as Orco lifted him off the ground by his throat. "You have the wrong one." Sal continued as he gasped for breath. "You've made my life a living hell." Orco fired back.

Gus handed Orco the scroll. "You're going after the wrong person."

Orco dropped Sal to the ground. Sal punched Orco in the stomach, who in turn, punched Reid in the colon, who punched Artesia and- crunch! His fist passed through Artesia's chest. Artesia rolled his eyes. "Don't worry about it."

A rat running on a treadmill in Artesia's chest snarled at Reid. Orco fumed at Reid. "We are in an all out-war because of you! We've already lost one of our own!"

Artesia sprayed breath freshener into his mouth, and then into his chest and under his arms. Sal turned to Reid. "You're the one, aren't you?"

"They've taken my girlfriend." Reid told him.

Sal took the scroll and looked it over. "Is that bird poop--?"

"Who do you have?" Orco asked him as Sal looked over Reid, checking him out from head to toe. He took out a stethoscope and checked his heart and then back and shoulders for scoliosis as he ran his fingers up his spine. "You look like you're doing okay. Might need to do an evaluation."

Reid began to walk back. "I am going back for my girlfriend.

You guys can do what you want, but I am not leaving her with those guys."

"Who?" Orco asked wondering who the others were and thinking back to when he got his assignment and the grim expectations. Reid stopped and turned around at the name that sounded familiar.

"Alastor Kowalski."

The words brought fear into the Death Squad's faces as Artesia dropped his whirring chainsaw and held up a finger as the pain quickly made its way up his leg. "I'll be back in a minute." He limped off.

Sal stood next to Reid. "Right kid, Alastor Kowalski. Fallen Angel. Damnation to all living and dead."

"Is that possible? Why would we go after him?" Pierrot asked as she pulled her hair back.

"That's why they were betting against you guys. They didn't intend on you coming back," Sal warned.

Orco looked as if he was going to pass out. "And he's our assignment."

"No wonder the snitch ran," Artesia commented as he tried on another pair of boots.

"We ain't leaving that girl behind," said Gus and Pervis threw up his arms, realizing that he was not quite done.

"What do I have to lose? What's it even matter? I'm stuck with you guys for a small eternity."

Orco turned to Sal. "They didn't think we could make it, huh?" Sal shook his head, "no."

"Anybody put their money on us?" Orco asked.

"Only one… Sorry." Sal told him as he prepared to train. "If we're gonna do this, we need to prepare for an all-out war." They all nodded in agreement. "What do we know about them?" Orco asked as the guys moved closer.

Reid stood in front of the group as he had their full attention. He pointed at a chalkboard with a large picture of the mansion and property on it. Pointing to the diagram, he said "They have security guards here, here, and here." He clenched his jaw and squinted his eye. "We need to be quick and precise."

The guys grappled with each other as Gus grabbed Sal in a headlock. "Here's the big chance you've been waiting on," Sal told him. Gus cranked harder on his neck but not enough to impress Sal. "Just a training exercise." Sal prodded him more. "Don't be a coward." Gus threw him to the ground, then pulled a feather out and Sal knocked his feet out from under him as he landed on his back with a thud. The group jogged around the cemetery as the hunchback blew his whistle and checked a stop watch. He shook his head in disgust.

Pierrot swung from a rope tied around a branch and over a tombstone. She ran to the next obstacle as Artesia wasn't so lucky and swung down but straddled the tombstone. He fell to the side and Stella was there to greet him with an ice pack. Orco attempted to swing down but the rope broke and he fell flat on the hunchback. The hunchback jumped up in his face and spoke with an assertive, gravely tone. "You're weak. Weak, I tells ya!" Orco, gripped with anger, broke a large branch in half with his bare hands. The hunchback tapped him on the chest. "On the inside."

Reid wrestled with the hunchback. The hunchback growled at him and then with a raspy voice- "You gotta want it, kid! You gotta want it more than the other guy!"

Gus threw a scissor kick at Sal, knocking him to the ground. Sal stood and dusted himself off. "Impressive." Gus looked for the next challenger for his patented scissor kick as the hunchback ran up and kicked Artesia in the groin. Artesia dropped to his knees and reached out for the ice pack.

"-the hell was that for?"

"Sorry, uh, got caught up in the excitement." The hunchback walked off and buffed the Death Mobile to a nice shine.

Orco stood on a large branch above the cemetery as the others looked up with eager anticipation. Orco flexed his broad wings and took a deep breath. It had always been his dream to fly. He reluctantly dove out and flapped his wings as hard as he could, briefly hovering above the group, who pulled desperately for him and watched in awe, until the wings gave out and he fell like a ton of bricks on top of the hunchback below.

They jogged around the cemetery and the hunchback checked

his stop watch. He nodded his head in approval.

Gus threw a scissor kick at Pervis, who ducked and went sailing over his head but came around again and connected, sending him reeling into a freshly-dug grave. Pervis pulled himself out with help from Gus as Orco grabbed some rope and his axe. "Let's desecrate the dead."

After a rigorous forty seven minutes of training, they were ready to face Alastor and his army of the dead.

WAR BETWEEN GOOD, SOMEWHERE IN BETWEEN, AND EVIL

Reece was tied up and dangling over a pit of bubbling green slime as blood-thirsty zombies circled her. Johnny the Weasel limped by, his ears were bright green and eyes glowing yellow. His possessed hand was in a small cage with a lock on it.

"Really not feeling too good," he complained.

A goon ran inside as Alastor leaned close to Reece and whispered in her ear. "It will all be over soon, my dear." He dipped his finger in the solution and ran it along his lips before licking it up and swallowing. A look of contentment streamed across his face. His eyes spun in his head and his head shook violently for a long three seconds before coming to an abrupt stop. His eyes landed on two pineapples as he pumped his fist with jubilation.

"Jackpot!! I think it's almost ready."

The goon moved straight to Alastor. "There's a guy at the gate." Alastor watched Reece with a hungry look in his eyes as he ran his tongue along his lips. He walked to the intercom while looking back as if he had seduced her. She avoided his look, squeezing her eyes shut and hoping she was back home in the Midwest.

Alastor punched the intercom. "We've been waiting." Nothing. He pushed it again. Static. He was about to punch it again when Reid came over the intercom cutting him off. "I've-"

Alastor hit it and cut Reid off. "Are you-" It was silent again as Alastor leaned close and then looked back at anyone for assistance. Artesia looked down from his position on top of the arch over the driveway and was ready to strike, but remained patient.

Inside the mansion, the scientist assisting Alastor leaned close.

"Hold it down." Reid shrugged his shoulders and looked back at the guys, who hid in the bushes as he was not sure what to do. Orco shook his head in disbelief as this was too typical. Reid pushed the button again. Alastor became impatient and shoved the scientist aside. "Get away from me."

He slowly and carefully pushed the button down and enunciated every word. "Where are your friends?"

"They're done with us. Just me."

BUZZZZZ! The gate opened and a pack of guards approached

with their guns drawn. Reid threw his hands up pretending to surrender.

"Guess what?" Reid asked. A guard signaled at him to move forward as Artesia dropped in front of the guard from the top of the wall above. Reid grabbed a metal rod sitting in the bushes and held it at his side. "It's payback time!"

Orco ran around the corner as the goons pointed their guns at them. "I'd put that gun away before someone gets a steel-tipped enema," Orco warned. They fired at Orco, who tossed the ace of spades tucked in his shoulder and it exploded in front of them, sending up a plume of smoke. Inside the mansion, Alastor leaned on the button and listened intently. He waved at the scientist. "Send them!"

Zombies were lined up in waves and marched down the hall, bumping into each other and moving toward the front door.

Orco grabbed a guard by the face and shoved him down. The guard giggled like a school girl and blushed. "I'll be good." Orco blew a fireball at the guards and they dodged it, rolling in the grass. A goon blasted off his machine gun and noticed Artesia, who smoked from the multiple bullets that screamed through his chest. Artesia rushed toward him and jerked the gun out of his hand "Why me? You couldn't find anyone else to hit?" The goon ran off and back to the mansion to warn Alastor as Zombies walked to them, led by the exterminator man whose eyes were milky and opaque. Green bile ran from his mouth. Reid backed off and worried more about Reece. "What the hell?"

Pervis studied the tall, thick concrete wall from the outside of the grounds. He ran alongside the wall trying to get up the nerve to go over and coached himself. "You can do this." He ran faster, picking up momentum to make the great leap. "All for good against evil. Save the PLANETTT!!!" He jumped up on top of the wall with his eyes closed and rolled over... To the wrong sprawling mansion.

The mood was sublime and playful. The bushes were sculpted into playful animals and the grass was colored pink. Girls played around the pool in bikinis. Pervis leaned up on his elbows to witness a pretty brunette in a bikini stop and wink at him. Another bikini babe stood over him and held a rifle in one hand. She helped him to his feet with her free hand.

"Are you okay?"

He stood up after dusting himself off and straightened his collar.

"This was all a test, wasn't it?"

A nice looking, older gentleman with a friendly, half-cocked smile, walked out to greet him. "Are you okay, son?"

Pervis observed the girls who splashed each other in the pool.

"I'm in heaven." He said to himself as the man slapped him on the shoulder and led him back to a table by the pool. "I would like to think so."

Terrified goons ran down the street and away from the mansion, hopping over fences and scrambling to get away. One goon grabbed a kid's bike after knocking him off and peddled away. An alarm rang on the grounds and Alastor spoke to Reece. "I think your friends are here."

Hundreds of zombies staggered outside, bumping into each other as they forged clumsily forward. A few zombies walked past the Death Squad and out onto the street, not quite sure what their assignment was.

Gus round-house kicked one and then another as Pierrot swung a club, knocking out dozens of them. Sal head-butted a zombie but it stood back up and he did it again but it slowly stood again. Frustrated, Sal flew off to another and it grasped onto a wing, flipping him over and bouncing him off the ground.

A net was dropped from a tree and fell over Pierrot, who swung wildy but quickly went down, caught up in the rope. Orco plowed through a handful of zombies but was shoved back by more. He was no match for the multitude of zombies that crowded around him. He waved his axe and sliced through a couple but more moved his way. Artesia was grabbed from behind as one chomped down into his head but spit it up and gagged.

"That'll teach ya!" Artesia bragged, but it bit his arms instead. "Owwwww!"

Orco, desperate and overwhelmed, blew fire but was met with a fire extinguisher sprayed into his mouth. He doubled over and coughed. The zombies surrounded the guys who were out of options, as Gus was still spinning around and kicking when he became dizzy and tired, and a large zombie simply shoved him over. They were surrounded and apprehended except for Reid, who threw his hands up in retreat. They slowly moved to him but he jumped one way and then the next and ran around them and into the mansion. The others were rounded up and taken to the mansion board room where Alastor sat patiently with his men.

Alastor stood as they approached and took off his mask, revealing that he was also an angel of death, which they already knew. His face was almost the same, only much older and a whiter shade of ghostly pale. He threw up his hands. "Surprise!"

World leaders stood against the wall and Orco scowled at them.

"You deserters."

A world leader shrugged it off. "If you can't beat em', join em'."

The others nodded in compliance. Alastor paced in front of Orco, obviously familiar with each other. "This isn't the army, Orco."

Orco looked around the room at the men in suits. "Who are the rest?"

"They're out there waiting for my cue. World leaders... Well known celebrities."

"Rock Gentry the action hero!?" Reid blurted out as he. Reid scooted around the room, dodging zombies. Rock lit up a cigar. "This has been a well-kept secret, so let's keep it that way," he winked.

"Thanks, kid."

Johnny the Weasel was green and his ears glowed. "I'm really not feeling too well," he complained.

The scientist drew the needle and tapped it a couple of times. Alastor waved over a guard and pointed at Johnny the Weasel.

"Lock him up, too."

Johnny stood straight up but held his aching stomach. "Wha-?"

"We needed a human, but you are part gorilla," Alastor told Johnny the Weasel, who scratched himself from head to toe.

"How do ya figure?"

Alastor strutted in front of the guys. "Didn't plan this out too well."

"As long as they take you out. That's all I want," Orco fired back but Alastor was undeterred and simply amused.

"Are you sure it's me you're after? I mean you guys are the joke of the afterlife."

Pierrot cracked her knuckles. "Let me at em, let me at em-" A demonic clown jumped in front of her and marked up her face to look like a clown, complete with a red nose. Artesia had a worried look on his face.

"I have a feeling I'm next."

A chainsaw buzzed and Artesia's arm was lopped off.

The guard scooted around to Johnny the Weasel just as a horse hoof clomped against the pavement of the driveway. More hoofs marched forward. A Japanese war dress swung behind a skeletal horse as it made its way up the driveway toward the mansion.

The intercom beeped and Rock walked to it to listen and Perneum's voice flowed out of the speaker. "I have a cheese pizza with extra fire. Name on the ticket is ***'The Death Squad'***."

Orco looked up as Artesia wedged a chimney poker where his arm used to be and Pierrot wiped off the makeup. Rock looked to Alastor for an explanation. "Extra fire? Death Squad?"

Johnny the Weasel, who was still on his knees and weary, tapped Alastor on the leg. "I know how you like pineapple on your pizza but-"

Alastor kicked him away. "Do I look like I'm in the mood for pizza, you ignorant baboon?" Alastor grimaced as he watched Johnny the Weasel's forehead expanding and contracting.

"Find out what is going on!" Alastor demanded as there were more thumps on the roof and they all looked up. Reece was lowered a couple of feet over the large vat of green bubbling toxin. She struggled to avoid the bubbles that splashed dangerously close to her face. "HELP!"

"I may not rule hell but I can rule earth. I will have millions of them," Alastor blew her a kiss. "Thanks to you, my sweet." and then to the group. "I almost didn't get to her in time." Alastor observed as he watched Reid climb around the side of the bubbling vat as a large blade swung back and forth above Reece. Alastor rolled his eyes. "What are you doing now?"

Reid jumped on the swinging blade, gripping the metal pole.

A zombie leaned over and shook the blade and Reece slid down further and hung on above the pit. Johnny the Weasel sat up. "You really don't want to get that stuff on you." He burped and a green cloud bellowed out then attacked his face, sending him back to the floor.

THUMP! THUMP! Could be heard from above. Alastor grabbed the vial of blood and the zombies stumbled out with their weapons drawn.

Meanwhile in Hell, Lucifer sat on a head in front of a big screen television and smashed a peanut down on another head. He took the peanut out and swiped away the shell on the ailing soul's head. "Guess what we're having next week?" The head looked up and he continued with a smile. "Oysters on the half shell." Lucifer laughed and looked over at the television which followed the action. "Let's see what you guys got." He cranked up the volume.

Perneum sat on one of the armored horses that flared its nostrils and led all the other Samurai warriors inside the gate. He raised his sword and they did the same, ready to fight. "Attack!" They followed him toward the mansion as zombies rushed out to do battle.

A zombie dragged himself to Orco and pointed his weapon when WHAM! Artesia slammed down on his head with his fist and hooked the gun, tossing it aside with the poker. Orco grabbed two zombies with his hulking arms and slammed their heads together. They crumbled to the ground, clutching their aching heads. Pierrot slammed Rock Gentry over the head and signaled at Artesia. "Let's go out and help the others."

BING! BING! A goon fired a couple of shots in the front yard at the approaching Samurai but it reflected off their iron shields. The samurai slammed his sword down on the gun. A fierce battle began with the clanging of armor.

Reid reached out to Reece and struggled to untie her as she dropped a couple more inches and the green slime almost touched her shirt and hair. Alastor ran down the hall and up the stairs to hide from the warriors who kept advancing forward.

Pervis sat in a lawn chair next door by the pool with the pleasant man who fired up a smoking pipe. The man motioned toward the mansion.

"They're usually pretty quiet next door."

He offered a pipe to Pervis who gladly accepted. "Neighbors?"

"They are always asking for a virgin and I don't know why." There was a brief silence as they watched the girls seductively rub suntan lotion on each other and giggle and then both broke down in knee slapping laughter.

Two goons came flying over the wall and two girls in bikinis holding flame throwers, torched them. One of them threw her long blonde hair back and pouted. "That's for knocking Bambi in the pool." Pervis and the man toasted each other with their cocktails as a zombie flew out of control and into the pool.

Samurai warriors and their horses ran through the yard kicking up dirt and grass and prepared for battle to the end. Alastor leaned out the window on the third floor. "No retreating! Stand up and fight!" He looked closer to see a limousine pulling in, then bit his fist and ran off to hide.

Alastor's plump wife, wearing gaudy jewelry and oversized sun glasses, got out of the limo clutching her bags, as a full scale war waged on in the front yard and the house. "Is this a party!? This better not be a party! I'll kick your butt, Al!"

Pierrot held her club as a zombie staggered her way. She spoke in a baseball announcer's tone and tapped the heels of her boots with it. "Top of the ninth and guess who's up to bat?" She gripped the club, clutched her groin and spit on the ground as a zombie staggered forward with his arms out. She swung the bat and knocked the zombie's head off his shoulders and sent it flying over the fence. "Pierrot, that's who!"

The head flew over the wall and rolled into a group of girls, who screamed. The head broke out into a smile. "Loved the May issue."

Alastor stretched his wings and started to fly, lifting himself a few feet off of the ground. Sal flexed his wings determined to capture him. "I'll go after him."

"No, he's mine." Orco grabbed Sal by the wing and twisted while pulling him away and Sal examined his broken wing. "I would have let you go after him… Honestly" Orco apologized and was already flapping his wings and slowly lifting himself off the ground. He took off running and flapping, slowly rising in the air but not quite high enough as he wrapped himself around a tree branch at the end of the property. He fought to break free from the branches that had become entangled around his arms and he gallantly leaped forward after tearing them away. His huge frame dipped down but went back up and he was moving forward and up again.

Orco was flying with all the determination he could find within himself. Alastor glided through the air but Orco was already catching up. Alastor looked back and flapped even harder but Orco tackled him in mid-air and they tumbled onto a nearby apartment complex rooftop.

"We could do this together." Alastor offered but Orco punched him across the chin as an old woman watered a dead garden on a patio below them.

"Can you take it somewhere else?" She complained as she watered a dead plant that wilted more under its weight.

Alastor went over the roof, but Orco caught him as he dangled over the edge. He was ready to pull him over when-- SLAM! Alastor smashed Orco's hand with a brick. "Arrgghh! You'll pay for this! All of this!"

"So, you want to earn your wings? Is it worth it?"

Orco pulled Alastor back but Alastor dropped the deadly vial toward the apartment below. Orco caught it, letting a drop of blood fall to the garden below but kept his grip on Alastor.

"They couldn't hold me, why should you?" Alastor bragged.

"You ran when people needed you... And tried to destroy the human race!" Orco remarked and Alastor thought about this for a second as they clawed at each other's eyes. "You should have given up a long time ago. You can't make up for the past."

Orco flexed his huge forearms and sent a hard punch to Alastor's ribs and followed it with an uppercut to the chin. "That's what I needed to hear."

Orco's wings stretched long and the flapping sent debris raining down on the woman who shook her fist at them. Alastor mocked him with sympathetic eyes. "Spark a little emotion, Tough Guy?"

Orco stood tall and towered over Alastor. "You want the good news or the bad?" Orco kneed Alastor in the stomach. "Now for the bad news." Orco flapped his large wings and crashed them into each other on Alastor's head. "POW!" Blackout. Orco grabbed Alastor by the collar and dragged him off of the roof.

The old woman looked at her garden, which bloomed in beautiful colors from the small drops of green ooze, but quickly snarled and violently bit at her.

VICTORY AT LAST

Back at the mansion things were returning to normal. Zombies dropped to the ground as other zombies walked down the driveway and back to their cemetery plots.

A realtor hammered a foreclosure sign in the front yard.

A glossy-eyed frat boy wearing a Hawaiian shirt and lei, staggered up to a zombie and leaned on him. "I know you! You were at the "End of the World" party-" He vomited down the zombie's leg. The zombie rolled his eyes knowing things couldn't get much worse. The frat boy straightened back up as much as his limp body would allow him and slapped the zombie on the shoulder. "You rock, dude." He offered a weak handshake. "Friends call me Wildman."

"Wildman" passed out and the zombie caught him and threw him over his shoulder, willing to walk him home.

Two Japanese Samurais held Alastor inside the mansion. Alastor tried to free himself and then coerce them into helping him. "How about the three of us go into business? Used car sales, not death. Oh, look s'mores."

They briefly looked away and Alastor broke free from the Samurais and dove into the pit of green slime leaving only a small splash behind him.

Alastor was gone and the police escorted out the last of the goons in hiding. They didn't even bother to ask questions and quickly fired up their squad cars and exited the property.

The guys stood around the death pit as Sal looked around the room.

"Now to find Roger Hughes."

Johnny the Weasel waved a finger from under the table. He spoke in a hoarse, raspy voice. "Did you say, Roger Hughes?" He picked himself up and leaned on the table. "Johnny the Weasel is my stage name. My real name is Roger Hu-"

Johnny collapsed, first hitting his chin on the table, and then going completely down. Sal rubbed his temples. "I think I need to get him to a doctor. Oh, yeah, I almost forgot something."

Sal signaled Gus to look toward a bubble of light that moved their way.

"I have someone I want you to meet."

A radiant elderly woman with curly brown hair and a warm smile, walked out of the light and hugged Gus.

"I'm counting on you to take care of the farm." She kissed him lightly as he could only stare with watery eyes and unable to move. He was paralyzed as the woman he had thought about day and night stood before him without a single worry. She ran her warm, transparent hand along his cheek. "You know where I'll be." She told him.

"I missed ya, Wanda... A lot.. A durn lot."

She smiled the smile that only someone who has seen the security and comfort that Heaven holds can smile and Gus grinned back relieved, knowing that she was in good hands and never far away.

Sal gave Gus a slight nudge. "You two might want a couple moments alone." Gus gladly obliged and followed her to the bubble holding her hand along the way.

Reece jumped in front of Sal. "What about my angel? I was the one in danger."

Sal led Reece to Reid. "Angels aren't always among the dead and you aren't Wallace, yet." The letters changed on the scroll to read Reece Wallace. Reid read it and then looked toward Sal as it started to become clearer. Reece would also soon be Wallace according to his destiny.

"I know what that means... I think," Reid paused, "Like, till death do us-"

"You two were meant for each other." Sal told him.

A huge, long multi-legged beast with Alastor's face, burst out of the pit and the group turned with swords, chainsaws, and guns blasting away.

Alastor, unconcerned and head smoking, grabbed a cocktail from the butler who stood patiently next to the pit. He downed the drink and followed it with a vile-smelling burp that spewed dark souls from his spacious mouth.

"We will meet again!" Alastor warned and then looked down on the butler after devouring the drink, glass and all. "A little too dry.

Cut back on the Vermouth."

More shots rang out as he dropped back in the pit and out of site. Orco leaned over to see nothing but a couple of bubbles make their way to the top in the middle.

Perneum turned to Orco. "Why didn't we ever have a butler?"

"Ya killed em'... All of em."

"Oh, yeah, that's right."

The butler quickly exited the room and crawled under the stairs, joining the hand.

THE DENOUEMENT (or resolution of the story)

Music played in the dance hall as people moved slowly around the room, grabbing refreshments and congratulating the group.

Reid was able to get the room for a reasonable price and decided to throw his saviors a party and more importantly, make Reece his wife.

A disco ball splashed bright colors on the crowd who stood below as Reid and Reece kissed a long, passionate kiss that would be the first of many. She tossed the bouquet behind her and Pierrot knocked all of the women aside with her hairy forearms and caught it, clutching it tightly.

Reid offered handshakes to everyone involved.

"Thanks for everything, guys... I can even overlook over the fact you wanted to kill me."

They gave him an *"oh, stop it"* gesture and congratulated each other. Artesia shook Perneum's hand. It was a moment that made Orco proud of his team. Satisfied, Orco began to walk away. "Time to cross over."

Reid grabbed him before he could escape. "No way, I'm dedicating a song to you guys."

Stella handed Artesia his arm. "My dad's a plastic surgeon." She looked him over and took some mental notes. "We can fix a few things."

Perneum raised his fist in victory. "I'm ready to take a few lives!"

Iris, pure and good angel, floated inside on the rays of a rainbow. She pinched Perneum on the cheek while floating beside him. "No, my ugly, little dwarf. You have all done well and have earned your wings."

"Who you calling a dwarf, you-?"

She put her hand to his mouth. "We've heard far too much from you already."

Iris waved her wand and they started to transform to radiant angels, (a temporary thing before they got their actual wings), but Orco told her to "stop." He signaled the group to join him on the dance floor. "Just one last dance for the boys… Girl."

Pierrot followed. "I'm game."

They lined up on the dance floor and struck a pose when the song ***"Disco Inferno"*** flowed out of the speakers. Orco was the first to move and the others followed with the rest of the party joining in.

The wedding and party were both a success as Stella and Artesia walked out of a building thinking they might be next to make the commitment.

Orco loaded up the Death Mobile which was covered by shaving cream when Pierrot walked over to him. Her red hair flowed with white flower petals, which danced around her head like a halo. "You look great!" He told her as she smiled and revealed jagged, decaying teeth and bad dental work. Orco cringed. "As opposed to, uh, how you looked earlier."

She pointed up and winked. "See ya up there."

A zombie took a long drag off a cigarette next to his grave. "Goodbye, cold, dark-" He fell into the grave and only the echo from below could be heard as he finished, "-world."

People lined the boulevard in Los Angeles. Samurai swordsmen and their horses trotted down the wide city street for a parade. A Samurai waved back at a child. They were followed by the Shriners in their go carts doing "crazy eights," with the go carts zig-zagging back and forth, narrowly missing each other.

The betting board showed the final odds on the "The Death Squad" at 8,597,498-1. God, always a great judge in character, smiled and counted his money. His faith in the Death Squad paid off in a big way.

A skeletal hand pulled on a coffin lid in the cemetery as creatures in the night laid down to rest. The lid slid over in DARKNESS and SILENCE.

THE END... for now. You know how these stories are, some sort of uprising in the near future.

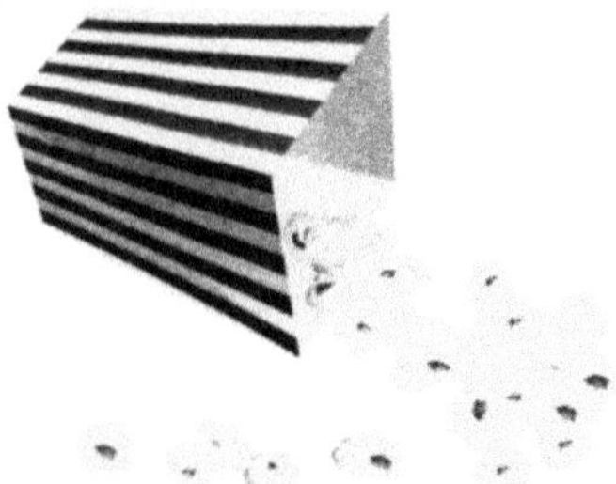

The DEATH SQUAD

www.ingramcontent.com/pod-product-compliance
Lightning Source LLC
LaVergne TN
LVHW010618160725
816125LV00011B/204
* 9 7 8 1 4 5 0 7 1 6 2 5 3 *